Bristol
OBSERVED

*Visitors' impressions
of the City
from Domesday
to The Blitz*

JH BETTEY

REDCLIFFE
Bristol

First published in 1986 by
Redcliffe Press Ltd,
49 Park Street, Bristol 1.

Reprinted 1989

© *J H Bettey*

ISBN 0 905459 65 2

Typeset by
Penwell Ltd, Parkwood, Callington, Cornwall
Printed by WBC Print, Bristol

CONTENTS

Acknowledgements

The assistance of several friends and colleagues who have helped by providing information, suggestions and illustrations is gratefully acknowledged. In particular, John Sansom and Mike Abbott of Redcliffe Press have made numerous useful comments and criticisms; the Librarian and staff of Bristol University Library have been unfailingly helpful, and have allowed me to use a number of illustrations from the University collection, and I am grateful for the advice of Mr George Mabey concerning the material in the University Archive collection; Michael Aston drew the plan showing the diversion of the river Frome in Bristol; the photographs owe much to the help and generosity of Jim Hancock and Gordon Kelsey. Frances Neale kindly allowed me to use some of her translations of William Worcestre's description and unique measurements of late-medieval Bristol.

J.H. Bettey

Introduction

This book describes the reactions of some of the innumerable visitors who have come to Bristol over the centuries, and their descriptions of the town, its buildings, industries, shipping and inhabitants. Their comments remind us of the hardships and dangers endured by travellers; they also illustrate their changing interests and observations and varied motives which had led men to travel.

Medieval travellers undertook their laborious journeys to an important port and manufacturing centre such as Bristol for business and profit, or they journeyed as pilgrims in search of spiritual gain, but they were seldom moved to leave detailed written descriptions of the places they visited, any more than they felt the need for accurate maps and plans, nor for sketches and illustrations of what they saw. It is his passionate interest in factual evidence and precise measurements which make the late-medieval traveller, William Worcestre, so extraordinary, and because he was a native of Bristol he naturally devoted a great deal of attention to the town and left a remarkable description of it. His meticulous concern for factual information and his descriptions of what he saw on various journeys through England make him the first of a long and distinguished line of local topographers and historians.

During the sixteenth century the peaceful, united land created by the Tudor monarchs, improved roads and a new approach to cartography all gave rise to a new breed of traveller who journeyed for pleasure and entertainment, to see the country and to enlarge his horizons, and who described what he saw in a spirit of patriotic pride in the diversity of the realm. The first of such travellers was John Leland who rode all over England during the reign of Henry VIII, at a time of great economic and social upheaval, when the ancient and wealthy monastic houses had just been swept away, many of their buildings demolished and their possessions scattered. Leland himself wrote to Henry VIII in 1543 explaining the reasons for his journeys,

> "I was totally enflammid with a love to see thoroughly al those partes of this your opulente and ample realme, . . . yn so muche that al my other occupations intermittid I have so travelid yn yowr dominions booth by the se costes and the midle partes, sparing nother labor nor costes, by the space of these vi. yeres

paste, that there is almoste nother cape, nor bay, haven, creke or peere, river or confluence of rivers, breches, waschis, lakes, meres, fenny waters, montaynes, valleis, mores, hethes, forestes, wooddes, cities, burges, castelles, principale manor placis, monasteries, and colleges, but I have seene them; and notid yn so doing a hole worlde of thinges very memorable."

Leland's comments on what he saw in Bristol are accordingly of great interest. But Leland and those who followed him were primarily interested in antiquities, in castles, churches and great houses, and in the important land-owning families. Later visitors were to have much more diverse interests. From the late sixteenth century more and more visitors described what they saw in Bristol, and only a few can be quoted. Some, such as Samuel Pepys, Daniel Defoe or Thomas Clarkson are so informative or memorable that they cannot be omitted. Others have been chosen to illustrate the development of the town, the trade of the port, the growth of the industries and the spread of Hotwells and Clifton. Visitors such as the remarkable and indefatigable traveller Celia Fiennes or the journalist Daniel Defoe were particularly interested in trade, industry and economic affairs, and with understanding the reasons for the rapidly-growing prosperity of Bristol.

The eighteenth century saw ever-increasing numbers of the new breed of tourists coming to Bristol. They came out of curiosity to see one of the richest towns in the country; they came to seek health or recreation at the Hotwells Spa and in the health-giving air of Clifton; others came to see the varied trades and industries or the great port with its far-flung markets of the second city in the kingdom, 'the metropolis of the west'. Some were people such as Alexander Pope, Horace Walpole or Fanny Burney with the leisure to record at length their impressions of Bristol and its suburbs. They were interested in the new merchants' houses like Clifton Hill House or Arnos Court, or in elegant gardens and grottoes like Goldney, and above all in the varied society who sought rejuvenation from the spa at Hotwells.

For descriptions of nineteenth-century Bristol great use has been made of an entirely different source, and extracts are quoted from the detailed evidence and reports of commissioners appointed by Parliament to enquire into all aspects of life and work in England. These provide a superb, authoritative and little-used source of local history, and deal with many aspects of life in Bristol which were ignored by well-bred and wealthy tourists.

The long tradition of English topographical writing and the description of local places, historic buildings and picturesque scenes was continued in the nineteenth and twentieth centuries with directories and tourist guides, but fewer travellers recorded their impressions of particular towns and their inhabitants. The greatest exception to this was J B Priestley who travelled through England in the autumn of 1933 and left an interesting record of his journey.

A shield from the present Guildhall (1843-45) reproducing a 13th century Bristol seal representing the castle and river.

7

ONE

MEDIEVAL VISITORS
'The Place of the Bridge'

The early origins of Bristol during the Saxon period are only slowly being revealed by archaeology, but by the time of the Norman Conquest in 1066 a small town, port and market was already established at this important crossing-point of the River Avon. Bristol was sited in a well-defended position, above the point where the river Frome joined the Avon, and where the two rivers provided a good anchorage for ships, well inland from the sea, safe from storms and pirates. By the year 1000 Bristol, which the Anglo-Saxon writers called 'Brycgstow' or 'the place of the bridge', had a mint and fortifications, and its inhabitants were engaged in overseas trade, notably with Ireland.

One of the earliest documentary references to a notable visitor to Bristol, and evidence for the importance of Bristol as a port, occurs in the Anglo-Saxon Chronicle for the year 1051. In that year Earl Godwine, Earl of Wessex, a leading figure at the court of King Edward the Confessor, raised a rebellion against the King. Godwine was supported by his four sons Earl Harold who was later to be King, Sweyn, Tosti and Leofwine. Their revolt was suppressed and Earl Godwine and his sons fled abroad; Sweyn, who was a seafarer, kept a ship at Bristol and it was this that was used by Harold and Leofwine to make their escape to Ireland where they sought refuge in Dublin. The brief entry in the Anglo-Saxon Chronicle reads

"1051

And Earl Harold and Leofwine went to Bristol to the ship which Sweyn had equipped and provisioned for himself. And the King sent Bishop Aldred from London with a force and they were to intercept him before he got on board, but they could not — or would not. And he went out from the estuary of the Avon, and had such stiff sailing weather that he escaped with difficulty, and he suffered great losses there. He continued his course to Ireland when sailing weather came".[1]

The event itself is not particularly important but it shows that Bristol was already a significant port, and the obvious starting

The old Bristol Bridge whose closely built shops and houses attracted many admiring comments until it was demolished in 1761.

point for a voyage to Dublin.

Soon after this incident, the connection between Bristol and Ireland gave rise to an angry protest from another important visitor to Bristol. This was St Wulfstan (died 1095), a bishop of the large diocese of Worcester which stretched right down the Severn, and throughout the Middle Ages included Bristol. Wulfstan's protest was made during one of his frequent episcopal visits to Bristol during the later eleventh century, and was over the trade in slaves which had become an important part of the traffic from Bristol to Dublin and other Irish towns. St Wulfstan's vigorous protest against this trade was recorded by William of Malmesbury, one of the most important of the monastic chroniclers of the Middle Ages, in a Life of St Wulfstan. William of Malmesbury, writing early in the twelfth century, described Wulfstan's protest as follows ;

"There is a maritime town called Bristol from which traffic goes by a direct route to Ireland, and so it is used to the

9

barbarity of that land. Natives of that town (Bristol) and others from England sail to Ireland for trade . . ."

(some sailors trading between Bristol and Ireland were caught in a storm, and were only saved from shipwreck by the miraculous intervention of St Wulfstan).

"Now this miracle made such an impression on the townsfolk of Bristol that nothing was more impressed on their minds than what he (Wulfstan) thought ought to be done. Following this, he removed from among them an ancient custom, which had so hardened their hearts that neither the love of God nor fear of King William had so far been able to abolish it. For many people, bought from all over England, were dragged off to Ireland in hope of greater profit; they offered for sale slave-girls, both virgins and those already with child. One could see and lament over the ranks of the poor wretches roped together, young people of both sexes, with the beauty of free men and unspoiled by age, who would be objects of pity to barbarians, they were daily exposed publicly for sale. An accursed deed, and infamous disgrace ! for those not mindful of their brutal condition to give over to slavery human beings... This very ancient custom, handed down in families from father to son, Wulfstan, as I have said, gradually abolished. Gradually, for knowing that their stiff-neckedness was not easily to be bent, he often stayed with them for two or three months, coming to that place (Bristol) every Sunday and scattering the seeds of his godly preaching, which grew with the passing of time so strong among them that not only did they put away that vice but they were an example to the rest of England to do the same . . ."

Through the powerful preaching of St Wulfstan the slave trade between Bristol and Ireland, which had given Bristol an unsavoury and sordid reputation, was eventually stopped.

The first visitors to Bristol who left any real account of the town were the Commissioners sent by William the Conqueror as part of the enormous task of compiling the Domesday Survey of 1086. It was when the royal court of William the Conqueror met at Gloucester for the Christmas festivities in 1085 that the King had 'deep speech' with his advisers and decided to send men all over England to collect information about the realm.

The anonymous Domesday surveyors who came to Bristol during

1086 described it in the terse and very technical latin of the Survey; the translation of their description is as follows:

"In Barton at Bristol were six hides. In demesne three carucates and 22 villeins and 25 bordars with 25 plough-teams. There are 10 serfs and 18 co-liberts having 14 plough-teams. There are 2 mills worth 140 shillings.

When Roger received this manor from the King he found there 2 hides and 2 plough-teams in demesne, and 17 villeins and 24 bordars with 21 plough-teams. There were 4 serfs and 13 co-liberts with 3 plough-teams.

In one member of this manor, Mangotsfield, are 6 oxen in demesne.

Of this land, the Church of Bristol holds three hides and has there one plough-team.

One radknight holds one hide and has one plough-team and 4 bordars with one team.

The manor and Bristol renders to the King 110 marks of silver.

The Burgesses say that Bishop G. (Geoffrey) has 33 marks of silver and one mark of gold on account of the King's ferm (Ferma unius noctis)."

The Domesday Surveyors describe the town of Bristol as part of the large royal manor of Barton Regis. Most of the manor was agricultural and was cultivated by various classes of tenants—villeins, co-liberts, bordars and serfs. Some land was held by Roger, possibly Roger of Berkeley, some by the Church in Bristol, and some by a radknight, an unusual class of freeman found most commonly in the Domesday Survey of the west midland counties. The principal person in the manor was however Bishop Geoffrey of Coutances, the half-brother of William the Conqueror who had amassed vast estates in south-west England. The Domesday entry for Bristol is not easy to interpret in detail, nor does it distinguish clearly between the port and the large manor of which it formed part. But the general implication is clear, the large sums due each year to the King show that Bristol was already a prosperous trading community, and was to be ranked among the most prosperous boroughs in the country.

In 1125 William of Malmesbury described the diocese of Worcester and the fertile vale of Gloucester which he would have known well; he also wrote of the numerous towns, villages and

11

abbeys along the valley of the Severn, and continued

> "In the same vale is the most celebrated town called Bristol, with a port, which is a commodious and safe harbour for all vessells, into which come ships from Ireland and Norway and from other lands beyond the seas."[2]

There is no mention of a castle at Bristol in the Domesday Survey, but it is unlikely that the Normans left such an important and strategic place undefended by a castle, and Bishop Geoffrey of Coutances and later Robert Earl of Gloucester seem to have been responsible for building a stone keep as well as other defences.

Certainly by the early twelfth century Bristol with its castle on the peninsula between the Avon and the Frome, together with its town walls was regarded as a very strongly defended place. During the reign of King Stephen (1135-1154) Bristol became the stronghold of Robert, Earl of Gloucester, half brother of the Empress Matilda. Matilda's claim to the English throne led to civil war throughout the reign of Stephen, a war which was waged especially fiercely in the west country, and was accompanied by pillaging, burning of towns, massacres and great suffering among the inhabitants. In this war Bristol played a major part as the headquarters of Matilda's forces under Robert Earl of Gloucester. It was in Bristol castle that Stephen passed his brief captivity in 1141, and there also the future King Henry II, who was eventually to restore peace to the land, spent part of his childhood. Our detailed knowledge of the events of the long war and of the suffering which it caused owes much to the fact that it was described in detail by two of the most famous of the medieval chroniclers of Wessex. An account is given by the distinguished twelfth century writer William of Malmesbury, and the events of the war are also described in detail by the anonymous author of *Gesta Stephani*, an account of the actions of King Stephen, possibly written by Robert of Lewes, bishop of Bath (1136-1166). He certainly knew Wessex well and describes the events which occurred in the region of Bath and Bristol in great detail. His work provides abundant evidence of the horrors of medieval warfare and of the suffering endured by the people of the district as fortune favoured first one side and then the other, and as undisciplined mobs of soldiers roamed the countryside. The author was a staunch supporter of Stephen's cause, and does not conceal his hatred for the followers of Matilda and especially for the Bristolians, as is shown in the following

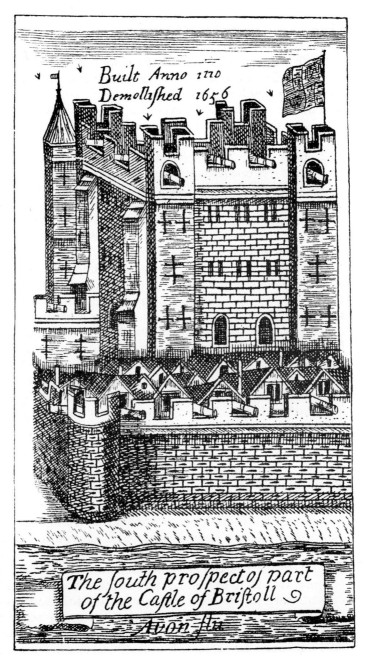

Built Anno 1110
Demolished 1656

The south prospect of part
of the Castle of Bristoll

Avon flu

The Great
Dungeon
Tower of
Bristol
Castle with
many
houses
clustered
within its
formidable
walls.

13

description of the misdeeds of the army which Robert Earl of Gloucester had assembled at Bristol in 1138.

"Bristol is well-nigh the most opulent city in the country; admitting merchandise by shipping both from the neighbouring and foreign parts; seated in a very fertile part of England, and, in point of situation, the most impregnable of all the English cities. For a certain part of the province of Gloucester, being narrowed in the form of a tongue of land, and stretched out at length, is washed on either side by two rivers; and these uniting in one large expanse of water on the lower side, where the ground itself declines, from the site of the city. A strong and forcible current of the sea also, flowing in abundance night and day, forces back the stream of these rivers on either side of the city, their reflux forming a wide and deep gulf, which affords a harbour of the utmost security, and well capable of holding a thousand vessels; and this embraces its circumference so nearly and closely that the whole city seems altogether to sink down upon the shores, and, as it were, to float upon the water. From one part of it, where it is accounted to be more open to attack, and more approachable, a fortress rises upon a lofty mound; and this being fortified by a wall, by bulwarks, and towers, and various engines, bids defiance to all attacks. Into this they collected such a great and wonderful crowd of horsemen and their train of footmen, nay, to speak more truly, a heap of highwaymen and robbers, that it appeared not only great and fearful to the beholders, but even horrible and surpassing belief. Having made their appearance, then, from different localities and places, they came thither in greater numbers and with greater joy; seeing that, under the command of a rich lord, and from out of a very strongly-defended castle, full permission was accorded them of doing as they listed in the most fertile district of England . . .

The men of Bristol then, with unbridled licentiousness, scoured the country with avidity and haste in every direction, when they heard of any lands or possessions which belonged to the king, or to those who were on his side, ravening like a pack of hungry dogs over the carcase which is laid before them. Yokes of oxen, flocks of sheep, whatever tempting object either their eye saw, or their proud heart desired, they seized and took away, sold, or consumed. When whatever was in their reach and compass had been brought into the pit of destruction, and utterly laid waste, if they heard of any rich or opulent persons in any part of England, they quickly attacked them, and either dragged them off by force, or beguiled them by treachery. They then bound up their eyes and gagged them, either with a lump of something forcibly thrust into their mouths, or with a little instrument made to fit the head, and furnished with teeth, after the fashion of a sharp cut curb or bridle, and so led them away with them blindfolded, and brought them into the middle of Bristol, like as we read of the sepulchre of Elisha; and, by means of either famine or torture, they forced from them everything they possessed, even to the last farthing. Others, devising a more wily piece of craft, in the parts where England was in more quiet state, where things were more peaceful, and the people were in greater ease and security, travelled from day to day, first in one direction, and then in another, over the most frequented roads, and assuming a false name, character, and business, making no show of arms, or presenting any remarkable appearance, and abstaining from the wicked and profligate language which is a characteristic of robbers, they put on a meek countenance and a quiet demeanour, and clothed their conversation with the garb of gentleness and humility. They thus showed themselves to be hypocrites of a new dye by their deceptive contrivances, until they achieved the object of their hopes, and led off to Bristol, that step-mother of all England, some rich man whom chance threw in their way, or who had been privily abducted from some place or other. This specious and deceitful mode of proceeding, this contrivance of hypocritical guile, increased to such an extent, in almost every corner of England, that there was scarcely a city or a village where they had not practised their villainous contrivances, or left some trace of this most iniquitous system of trickery. Hence there was no possibility of travelling the king's highways with the accustomed degree of security; no man could place confidence in his fellow as he had been wont; but wheresoever one person saw another, in the course of his journey, he immediately began to tremble all over, and timorously avoided his glance, and either took refuge in an adjoining wood, or turned some other way, until he could pluck up spirit to pursue his journey with some degree of safety and courage . . ."[3]

During the reign of Henry II (1154-1189) and of his sons, Richard I (1189-1199) and John (1199-1216), the great stronghold of Bristol castle was one of the principal royal castles in England. Henry III (1216-1272) spent lavishly on the improvement of the castle, including the building of a new hall and gate tower, and it was in the keep at Bristol castle that the unfortunate Princess Eleanor of Brittany spent her long imprisonment in England until her death in 1241. Princess Eleanor was the sister of King John's nephew Arthur of Brittany; Richard I had intended that Arthur should succeed him, and Arthur was brutally murdered by John's men in 1203. Bristol castle was used as a safe, reliable prison for Arthur's sister, the young princess Eleanor, thus ensuring that she could never marry or produce an Angevin heir to the throne to rival the Plantagenets represented by King John and his son Henry III. For the rest of her life Eleanor remained a prisoner at Bristol castle, and after her death in 1241 her body was taken to the nunnery at Amesbury for burial.

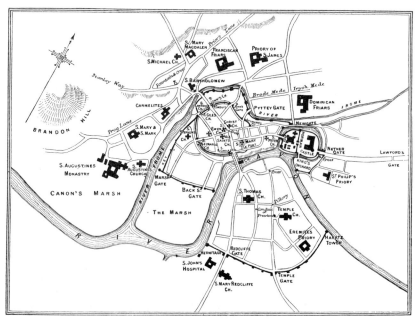

Bristol in the 13th century showing the full extent of the City Walls and the ancient churches and religious houses.

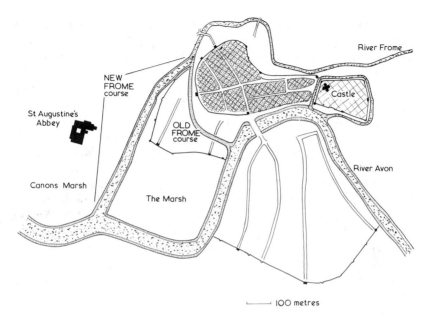

Between 1239 and 1247 the River Frome was diverted along a freshly cut channel, thus ensuring Bristol's future as a major port in the coming centuries.

During the later Middle Ages, as Bristol grew in prosperity and developed in size, becoming one of the principal ports of the Kingdom, there was no lack of distinguished visitors to the town, but few of them left any record of what they saw or of their impressions of Bristol or Bristolians. Charters and liberties were granted or confirmed to Bristol by many of the late medieval Kings, and many of them spent time in the town. An important charter was granted to Bristol by Henry II in 1155, and another by the future King John in 1188, the year before his accession to the throne. John came frequently to Bristol on his constant journeyings around England, and was at Bristol Castle at least once in every year between 1204 and 1210. For a time he kept his treasury in the strong keep at Bristol. Further charters were granted to the town by Henry III, and it was during his reign that the growing trade of the port of Bristol, especially the export of wool, cloth, ropes, sailcloth and lead and the import of wines, led to the decision to create a new, improved harbour for large ships by diverting the course of the river Frome. By about 1240 the port facilities of

Bristol were inadequate to cope with the shipping needed for the rapidly expanding trade, and the improvement which was undertaken is one of the most remarkable examples of civic engineering in the whole country. The quay on the Avon was small and inconvenient, and at low tide ships were left stranded on the stony bottom of the river and suffered damage to their timbers. The ambitious task was therefore undertaken of diverting the tributary river, the Frome, from its original course, just south of and parallel to Baldwin Street, into a new and deeper channel across the marsh, some 750 yards long. This provided at the new confluence with the Avon stone quays a soft muddy bottom for ships to lie on when the tide went out. The new channel also made it easier to turn ships. The work was done during the years 1239-1247 at the enormous cost of £5,000. This far-sighted piece of civic enterprise did much to establish the prosperity of the port of Bristol during the following centuries, and the Frome still flows along its thirteenth century channel to join the Avon. The enterprise was encouraged by the Crown, and a writ of Henry III, issued in 1240 refers to the new development and commands the men of the growing suburbs of Redcliffe to join with the men of Bristol in carrying out and finishing the work from which both will benefit,

"27 April 1240

Henry, by the grace of God, King of England . . . to all worthy men dwelling in Redcliffe in the suburb of Bristol, greeting.

Whereas our beloved burgesses of Bristol for the common good for the whole town of Bristol as of your suburb have begun a certain trench in the Marsh of St Augustine that ships coming to our port of Bristol may be able to enter or leave more freely and without impediment; which trench indeed they will be unable to perfect without great costs. We command you that, whereas from the betterment of the same port not only to the burgesses themselves but also to you, who are partakers of the same liberties which our aforesaid burgesses have in the town aforesaid and in scot and lot you are fellows with them, no little advantage ought to accrue. Moreover, it may be very useful and fruitful for you for the work of the trench aforesaid to be perfected successfully according as it concerns you together with our aforesaid burgesses, to whom as sharers in the liberties aforesaid you shall give like efficacious aid as they themselves do, lest the aforesaid work, which we regard as our

18

own, through your defection should receive delay.

Witness myself at Windsor on the 27th day of April in the twenty-fourth year of our reign."[4]

Edward I (1272-1307) also visited Bristol frequently, and Bristol castle played an important part in the conflicts between the barons and the Crown during his reign, and during the troubled reign of Edward II (1307-1327). In 1327 Edward II was imprisoned in Bristol castle by his queen, Isabella, and her lover, Mortimer; later the king was moved to Berkeley castle where he was hideously murdered on 21 September 1327, an incident commemorated in horrific detail by one of the roof-bosses in the north transcept of Bristol cathedral.

An unwelcome visitor of a quite different kind came to Bristol during the winter of 1348-49. This was the Black Death which entered England by way of the Dorset port of Melcombe Regis in the summer of 1348 and spread rapidly through Dorset and Somerset reaching Bristol by the autumn. This fearsome plague struck indiscriminately at all classes and all ages; its impact was sudden and rapidly fatal. Henry Knighton, a monk of Leicester recorded in his Latin Chronicle for 1348-49

"Then the dreadful pestilence . . . came to Bristol, and there died almost all the strength of the town, suddenly overwhelmed by death, for there were few who were sick for more than three days, or two days or half a day. Then this cruel death spread everywhere, following the course of the sun."[5]

There is no way of knowing the death-rate suffered in Bristol during the onslaught of the plague. A list of the town council for 1349 names fifty-two dignitaries, and of these fifteen have been struck through to indicate that they were dead. This represents a death-rate of nearly 30 per cent, and compares with a death-rate among the clergy in Somerset during the plague of nearly 48 per cent. The toll was no doubt a good deal higher in the insanitary crowded dwellings of the poor, the mariners and the industrial workers in Bristol.

Among the most significant of all the medieval visitors to Bristol were the commissioners and representatives appointed by the Crown and by the counties of Gloucestershire and Somerset in 1373 to establish and set out the boundaries of the newly-established county of Bristol. Until 1373 the busy and developing port of Bristol remained divided for purposes of local government and

19

justice, the ancient town and castle being part of Gloucestershire, while the prosperous suburbs of Redcliffe and Temple Fee south of the Avon were part of Somerset. In 1373 when Edward III (1327-1377) was in desperate need of money to carry on the Hundred Years War against France, the payment of 600 marks (£370) secured for Bristol a Charter granting it the status of an independent county, the first provincial town to be created a county.

"8th August, 47 Edward III, (1373)

Edward, by the grace of God, King of England and France and Lord of Ireland, to Archbishops, Bishops, Abbots, Priors, Dukes, Earls, Barons, Justices, Sheriffs, Reeves, Baliffs, Ministers and all other his faithful people, greeting. Know ye that whereas . . . divers liberties and quittances have been granted for ever to our beloved burgesses of our town of Bristol and their heirs and successors . . . we, at the supplications of our beloved Mayor and commonalty of the town aforesaid, truly asserting the same town to be situate partly in the County of Gloucester and partly in the County of Somerset. We have granted and by this our charter have confirmed for us and our heirs to the said burgesses and their heirs and successors for ever, that the said town of Bristol with its suburbs and the precinct of the same according to the limits and bounds, as they are limited, shall be separated henceforth from the said Counties of Gloucester and Somerset equally and in all things exempt, as well by land as by water, and that it shall be a County by itself and (be) called the County of Bristol for ever; . . ."

The Charter went on to describe in great detail the government of the new county of Bristol, its relationship with the central government and its powers and jurisdiction. The Crown also appointed commissioners, among them the bishop of Bath and Wells, the bishop of Worcester, the abbot of Glastonbury and the abbot of Cirencester, who were to visit Bristol, and, together with representatives from Gloucestershire and Somerset, were to set out clearly the boundaries of the new county. The boundaries included all Bristol's suburbs, and extended down the Avon and into the Bristol channel as far as the islands of Steep Holm and Flat Holm.

For visitors to Bristol during the late Middle Ages the *Kalendar* started by the town clerk Robert Ricart in c.1479, and which also records some earlier events in Bristol history, is an invaluable source. From this we learn that Henry VI (1422-1461) came to Bristol in 1447 'and was there worshipfully receyved', and that he came again in 1448. In 1461 Edward IV (1461-1483) visited Bristol, and Ricart records:

"This noble prince Kyng Edward the fourthe in the first yere of his reigne came first to Bristowe, where he was ful honourably receyvid in as worshipfulwise as evir he was in any towne or citee."

From other sources we also learn that on this visit Edward IV was entertained by the wealthy Bristol merchant William Canynges in his fine house at Redcliffe overlooking the harbour with 'a stone tower of great beauty with many rooms and four bay-windows.' In 1476 Edward IV came again to Bristol and stayed at the abbey of the Augustinian canons whose church was later to become the cathedral of Bristol. Ricart describes this visit in his *Kalendar* as follows:

"This yere cam Kyng Edward that noble prince to Bristowe, and lodged in the Abbey of Seynt Austins. And the same tyme he had of th'inhabitants of this Towne and of the contreyes adjoyning a grete benivolence of money gyven hym, to sustentacion of his werres (wars)."

Ricart also records the great and destructive storm and floods which occurred in the Bristol region during October 1484:

"This yere, the XVth day of October, was the grettest flode and the grettist wynde at Bristowe and in the cuntrey there abouts that ever was seen, and grete hurt doon in the merchaunts' sellers in wode (woad) and salt; shippes lost at Kyngrode, the Anthony of Bristowe and a ship of Bilbowe set a-land at Holow bakkes, and other botes and cokkes lost; saltmarsh drowned, corne, catell, and houses borne away with the sea, and moche people drowned, to the nommebre of C.C. (200) and more."

In 1486 Henry VII (1485-1509) and his queen Elizabeth came to Bristol with a large number of courtiers and were entertained in the town. The visit was marked by various civic celebrations, the bishop of Worcester preached before the royal party on College Green, and the King and Queen went on pilgrimage to St Anne's chapel in the wooded valley of the Avon at Brislington, a noted shrine and place of pilgrimage for Bristolians.

A contemporary account of Henry VII's visit in 1486 records that

21

the King came from Gloucester to the abbey of Kingswood where he stayed for the night, and the next day he dined with Sir Robert Poyntz at Iron Acton, before coming on to Bristol. At Lawford's Gate the King was welcomed by the Mayor and Burgesses, all on horse-back, and was then greeted by processions of the friars and of the various Bristol parish churches. The King then entered Bristol where he was met by a series of pageants, 'with great melodie and singing', and by a succession of long verse speeches of welcome. At the High Cross the King was entertained by 'a pageant ful of mayden children richly dressed', and at St John's Gate there were further speeches of welcome.

"And a littell further ther was another pageant of an Oliphante (elephant) with a castell on his bakk curiously wrought, the Ressurection of Our Lorde in the highest tower of the same, with certeyne Imagerye smytyng Bellis, and al went by Weights mervelously wele done".

Having admired the elephant and his clockwork burden, the King moved on across the Frome to College Green. We get some idea of the small, intimate nature of town at this time with its narrow streets and overhanging houses, and of the kind of welcome the King received, from the fact that as he passed along one of the streets a baker's wife leaned out of an upper window and sprinkled a handful of wheat upon him, crying 'Welcome and Good Luck'. On College Green the King was received by the solemn procession of the Abbot and Canons of St Augustine's abbey where he stayed during the three days of his visit.

Henry VII's reception in Bristol illustrates the essential link between the Church and the Community in the town during the later Middle Ages, for the King's stay in Bristol coincided with the popular religious festival of Corpus Christi, and the highlights of his visit consisted of his participation in the religious procession through the streets and attendance at an open-air sermon on College Green at which the Bishop of Worcester preached. All this is in marked contrast with the well known visit of Henry VII's grand-daughter, Queen Elizabeth, who came to Bristol in 1574, but whose lavish reception was essentially civic and secular.

In 1497 Bristol was threatened with an unwelcome and quite different sort of visitation. In that year a large number of Cornishmen rose in revolt against the heavy taxes imposed by the Crown. Under their leader, a blacksmith from St Keverne called

Michael Joseph, they marched on London and were eventually defeated by the King's forces at Blackheath. On their way to London they came to Wells, and attempted to enter Bristol to demand food and lodging, but they were refused entry by the Mayor. Ricart, no doubt greatly exaggerating the numbers involved, recorded the event as follows:

"1497 John Drewes, Mayor.

This yere the Cornyshmen rebelled ageynst the King, and the Lord Awdley arose with them. And the King met with them at Blak heth, and there had victory of his enemyes rebelles, and the said lorde Awdley was taken ther and behedded at Tower Hill. The same lord when he was at Wells with the blak smyth called Migheli Josef, Capteyn of the Cornysh men, havyng with them 40,000 men, sent to the Maire of Bristowe to ordeign lodgyng and vitaill for 20,000. But the Maire sent them word that they shuld come no nere, and if they wold come ner, at their owne adventur. And then the Maire mustred and made redy to withstond the said rebelles, and garnished the town walles with men harnessid and with gonnes, and brought

An imaginary portrait of William Worcestre, born in Bristol in 1415, the father of English topography.

23

shippes and botes about the mersshe, garnisshed with men, artillery, and gonnes. And the said rebelles hereng of this chaunged theire purpose and tooke another wey."[6]

By far the most informative of all medieval visitors to Bristol was William Worcestre, whose account of his journeys around the country and detailed observation and measurement of buildings, streets and other features of towns provide an outstanding source for late medieval topography and architecture. His careful record of what he observed makes him the earliest of a long line of English travellers who set out to provide a detailed description of the country, and he is the pioneer of English antiquarian and topographical writing. William Worcestre's account of Bristol is especially detailed since he was himself a Bristolian, and he had a house in the town. He was born at Bristol in 1415 and educated at Oxford; he entered the service of Sir John Fastolf whose widespread estates included the highly profitable cloth-making village of Castle Combe in Wiltshire as well as extensive lands in Norfolk and elsewhere. He undertook many journeys and commissions on Fastolf's behalf, and was intimately concerned with the management of his estates. After Fastolf's death in 1459 Worcestre acted as one of the executors of his long and complex will. It was during the decade before his death in about 1485 that William Worcestre made the journeys which resulted in his antiquarian and topographical writings, and his main journeys were undertaken in the years 1478 and 1480. William Worcestre's detailed account of late medieval Bristol, street by street, with details of churches, chapels, the castle, houses, streets, lanes and even cellars, written mostly in his own curious Latin, has never been fully published in translation, although an edition is in preparation.

Worcestre carefully described the streets and lanes of the town, including the gate by St Leonard's church leading into Baldwin Street which curved around the old town centre following the earlier course of the river Frome, Pill or Pylle Street which led to the Quay past the fine new tower of St Stephen's church, the Back (now Welsh Back) with its slipways, shipping and washerwomen, Wine Street with the Pillory, Broad Street, Corn Street, Marsh Street where many merchants and mariners lived, and College Green which then as now was a distinctive triangle of open land. A remarkable and highly unusual feature of Worcestre's work is that he was fascinated by the measurement of buildings and everywhere took the trouble to record meticulously the dimensions of streets, bridges, churches and other buildings. For example he tells us that 'the length of the whole church of St Mary Redcliffe, except the Lady Chapel, is 63 yards. The length of the Lady Chapel is 13 yards 1½ feet, and its breadth 7 yards; the breadth of the whole church is 18 yards, the total length of Redcliffe church is 77 yards.' Likewise we are told that the tower of St Mary Redcliffe is 300 feet high 'of which 100 feet have been cast down by lightening'; and that 'the length of Bristol Bridge is 140 steps'. Worcestre measured the length of Bristol Back (now Welsh Back) and found it to be 240 of his steps or paces, similarly he found that 'the length of the parish church of All Saints Bristol measures 74 steps. Its breadth measures 33 steps.' By All Saints' church he measured the width of the street (now All Saints Lane) which he found to be 5 yards, and he also noted that 'there are one or two cellars for the sale of wine in the said small road'. He described the tower of St Stephen's church with its ornate decoration and elegant stonework, St John's church and the gateway beneath leading from the Quay to Broad Street, the church of St James, the crypt of St Nicholas, and St Augustine's abbey. He also obtained from the porter or gatekeeper at Bristol Castle details and measurements of the building, with its great walls, towers and defences.

William Worcestre also went to Brislington where he visited St Anne's Well, a famous place of pilgrimage for Bristolians and for many others who came long distances to worship in the chapel there. Worcestre measured the chapel and also described the two huge candles which were provided each year for the shrine by the guilds of Cordwainers and Weavers, and the little models of ships hanging in front of the image of St Anne.

William Worcestre wrote his account of Bristol only a few years after the death of the great Bristol merchant William Canynges who died in November 1474, and while the memory of Canynges' wealth, charities, and munificence in Bristol were still fresh in men's minds and while his numerous ships were still trading from the port of Bristol. No doubt with some exaggeration concerning the numbers of sailors and craftsmen who were employed, William Worcestre recorded the following details about Canynges:

"Sir William Canynges, who was Mayor of Bristol five times, for 8 years had 800 men at work on ships and had labourers, carpenters, masons and others, 100 men a day.

Of ships he had:
The Mary Canynges of 400 tons
The Mary Redcliffe of 500 tons
The Mary and John of 900 tons burthen cost him in all 4000 marks (£2,666 13s. 4d.)
The Galiot, a ship of 50 tons burthen
The Cateryn, of 140 tons burthen
The Marybat, of 220 tons burthen
The Margaret of Tynly, of 200 tons burthen
The Little Nicholas, of 140 tons burthen
The Katheryn of Boston of 220 tons burthen
The . . . ., a ship lost off Iceland, of about 160 tons burthen."[7]

Worcestre also described the fine house in which Canynges had lived on the Back behind Redcliffe Street looking down on the river, with a tower, fine bay windows and highly decorated rooms. A sumptuous and appropriate dwelling for such important Bristol merchant and benefactor.

William Worcestre's detailed and carefully measured descriptions of churches, streets and buildings provide a remarkable picture of Bristol at the close of the Middle Ages, before all the changes of the sixteenth century which were to have such an effect upon the appearance of the town.

Notes

1. David C Douglas and G W Greenaway, eds., *English Historical Documents*, 11, 1953, p.123-4.
2. N E S A Hamilton, ed., William of Malmesbury's De Gestis Pontificum Anglorum, *Rolls Series*, 1870, p.292.
3. K R Potter, ed., *Gesta Stephani*, 1955, p.37.
4. N Dermott Harding, ed., Bristol Charters 1155-1373, *Bristol Record Society*, 1, 1930, p.19.
5. Henry Knighton, Chronicon, *Rolls Series*, 92, II, p.59.
6. L Toulmin Smith, Ricart's Kalendar, *Camden Society*, N.S. V, 1872.
7. J H Harvey, *William Worcestre—Itineraries*, Oxford, 1969.

Other Sources

David Walker, *Bristol in the Early Middle Ages*, Bristol Historical Association, 1971.
H A Cronne, ed., Vita Wulfstani, *Camden Society*, XL, 1928, 43, 91.
J W Sherborne, *The Port of Bristol in the Middle Ages*, Bristol Historical Association, 1965.
Bryan Little, *The City and County of Bristol*, 1954.

TWO

THE TUDOR PERIOD
'A Noble Town of Grete Trade'

The wealth and importance of Bristol during the sixteenth century, as a port, as a manufacturing centre, and as the focal point for a large part of the west of England, meant that an ever-increasing number of visitors came to Bristol, and many left accounts of what they saw and of their impressions of the town. Visitors included members of the Tudor royal family, merchants, traders, explorers, mariners, and others who came purely from a desire to see the different parts of their own country. A growing feeling of national pride and patriotism fostered a market for books of travel and descriptions of England, and amid so many other new developments, the sixteenth century also saw the beginnings of the great English tradition of topographical writing.

One visitor who left no account of his impressions of Bristol, but whose visit was to have the most profound and far-reaching effects, was John Cabot, a citizen of Venice, who came to Bristol in 1495, no doubt drawn by the growing reputation of Bristol seamen and navigators in seeking new lands and new markets beyond the seas. In a remarkably short time Cabot was able to win the respect and confidence of hard-headed Bristol merchants and persuade them to provide him with a small ship the *Matthew* and a crew of eighteen men in order to search for new lands to the west across the unknown waters of the Atlantic Ocean, in the hope of finding a new and shorter route to the riches of the East.

Cabot sailed from Bristol on May 2nd 1497, and on June 14th, after fifty-two days at sea, he and his crew landed upon the territory which they were to call the 'New Found Land'; the first definite landing of an English crew upon north American soil, and a discovery, which although not fully appreciated at the time, was to have momentous consequences for England and for Bristol. Upon his return to Bristol on August 6th 1497, Cabot was rewarded with a gift of £10 and a pension of £20 a year from King Henry VII; the royal bounty was paid to Cabot from the customs receipts of the port of Bristol by the royal 'Customer' or official who was a Bristol merchant called Richard Ameryke, and whose name may in some unknown fashion have become attached to the New World.

John Cabot made further voyages of exploration from Bristol, seeking for a sea-route to the East, and in 1509 his son, Sebastian Cabot, sailed from Bristol with a large contingent hoping to find a north-west passage to Cathay and the Indies. These voyages, and many others which followed, were to link Bristol's fortunes to the trade and colonisation across the Atlantic, and were to have immense and far-reaching consequences for the fortunes of the port.

The rewards of exploration were to be realised during the seventeenth and eighteenth centuries, but meanwhile the traditional trade of the port of Bristol with the European mainland, with Ireland and with the Mediterranean continued to provide the town with its principal livelihood throughout the sixteenth century. Bristol remained very small by modern standards, probably reaching no more than 12,000 inhabitants by the end of the sixteenth century, and with settlements still clinging very tightly to the small area of the walled medieval town. In 1540 one of the earliest of the English topographers, Richard Barlow, a Bristol merchant who had been a resident in Spain and who had spent several years in travel and overseas adventures, described Bristol almost entirely in terms of its shipping, although like others, he was also greatly impressed by Bristol bridge. This was the splendid medieval bridge over the Avon, built during the thirteenth century, with houses four or five stories high on either side of it. Across the centre of the bridge, with the road passing underneath it was the Chapel of the Assumption of the Blessed Virgin. The whole bridge with its fine architecture, shops and houses, reminded visitors of the similar, though larger, bridge across the Thames in London. It remained the principal entrance to the town until it was demolished and replaced by a wider, more serviceable but much less picturesque bridge in 1761. In *A Brief Summe of Geographie* Barlow described Bristol as

". . . a noble towne of grete trade and many shippes belonging to it. It hath a goodlie haven that cometh through the towne and a sumptuouse bridge over it of lyme and stone after the maner of the bridge of London. The shippes and botes comen in to ii partes of the towne, the one is called the Backe, the other the Key, and ii leagues from the towne is the river of Severne, ther is a goodlie rode called Kyngrode and another within that called Hungrode, wher ryde the shippes that liste not to come before the towne."

Barlow's main object in writing was to encourage further overseas exploration, and he commented sadly upon the major part played by Bristol in the early voyages of discovery and upon what he regarded as the lack of enterprise which had been shown by Bristol merchants in exploiting the possiblilities of the new lands. In his description of Newfoundland he wrote of

". . . the New Founde lande which was fyrst discovered by marchants of Brystowe . . . But whereas our Englishe marchantes of Brystowe dyd enterpryse to discover and discovered that parte of the land, if at that season they had folowed toward the equinoctiall, no dowt but they shuld have founde grete riches of gold and perle as other nations hath done sence that tyme."[1]

Bristol was also visited during the late 1530s by the most famous of all sixteenth century topographical writers, John Leland. In 1533 Leland began to travel the whole country, making copious notes of all he saw; and as he explained to Henry VIII in 1543, he 'was totally enflammed with a love to see thoroughly al those partes of this your opulente and ample realme . . .' On Leland's death in 1552, his proposed *Description of the Realm of England* was still not complete, and his notes remained confused and unpublished until the eighteenth century.

Leland's work, however, provides the fullest and most detailed picture we have of England during the reign of Henry VIII, a priceless record of the face of the country at a time of great change. Leland journeyed to Bristol from Bath, riding through Kelston, Bitton and Hanham. At Hanham he may have stayed with Sir John Newton at Barrs Court which he decribes as 'a fayre olde mannar place of stone caullyd Barrescourte'. The rough, uncultivated land of the forest of Kingswood stretched to the very edge of Bristol and Leland wrote "From Barrescourte onto Bristow a 3 myles by hilly and stony ground withe fern over growne in divers placis". Of Bristol, which he described variously as Bristow or Brightestowe, Leland wrote voluminous notes, describing the site of the town between the Avon and the Frome, with its strong walls and the town gates each with a parish church over or beside it—St John's gate, St Leonard's gate and St Nicholas's gate. He lists also eight other parish churches which were crowded into the small area

Map of Bright-stovve by Hoef-nagle, 1581.

30

31

within the walls—St Lawrence, Christ Church, St Ewen or Audoen, St Werborow or Werburgh, All Saints or All Hallows, St Mary Port, St Peter and St Stephen with its fine tower 'right highe and costly'. The great castle continued to dominate the whole town, and remained a strong and impressive fortress, even though some parts had been allowed to fall into decay.

> "In the castle be 2 courtes. In the outer courte as in the northe west part of it is a great dungeon tower, made as it is sayde of stone brought out of Caen in Normandye by the Red Earl of Gloucester. There be many towres yet standinge in both courtes, but all tendithe to ruine."

Leland also commented upon the former religious houses in Bristol which had recently been dissolved, and upon the former house of the Augustinian canons which had been converted into the cathedral of the newly-formed diocese of Bristol in 1542. He noticed the numerous pipes or conduits which brought water to all parts of the town, and Bristol bridge 'the grete bridge of 4 stone arches over Avon'.

Leland provides a charming and informative note on the harbour, and on the way in which it had been improved during the thirteenth century by altering the course of the river Frome,

> "The Haven of Brightestowe
>
> The shipps of old tyme cam only up by Avon to a place called the Back where was and is depthe enowghe of watar; but the botom is very stony and roughe sens by polecye they trenchid somwhat a-lofe by northe west of the old key on Avon anno 1247 and in continuance bringyng the course of Frome ryver that way hathe made softe and whosy harborow for grete shipps."[2]

In the summer of 1535 King Henry VIII with his Court had intended to visit Bristol, but was deterred from coming by an onslaught of plague in the town, a common hazard in the crowded and insanitary conditions of sixteenth century town life. Instead the King stayed at Thornbury where he and his Queen, Anne Boleyn, were presented with lavish gifts by the Mayor and Corporation of Bristol. Ricart's *Kalendar* records that the leading figures of Bristol went to Thornbury and

> ". . . presented unto the kynges high majestye x fatte oxen and xl shepe towards his most honorable household, and to the right excellent Quene Anne one cuppe with a cover of silver

overgilt, weighing xxvii unces, with c marks of gold within the same cuppe, as a gifte of this the kynges Towne and her Chambre of Bristowe, her grace then promysing to demaund or have noon other gifte but oonly that, if her said grace wold resorte to this said Towne at any tyme thereafter.''

In fact Anne Boleyn was executed in May 1536 and made no more demands upon the Mayor and Corporation of Bristol.

Already by the time of Henry VIII's visit to Thornbury in 1535, Bristol was racked with the bitter theological controversies that accompanied all the changes of the Reformation. The important town and seaport of Bristol, with a strong tradition of religious nonconformity dating back to the days of John Wycliffe and the Lollards more than a century before, was visited during the 1530s by a succession of popular preachers, both reformers and conservatives, and their fierce debates, conducted from rival pulpits, provoked violent religious divisions and dissent throughout the town.

Among the visiting preachers was Hugh Latimer who later became bishop of Worcester, and was to be one of the leading English reformers and a celebrated preacher. In 1533 when he came to Bristol, Latimer was rector of West Kington west of Chippenham and some 12 miles from Bristol; his powerful preaching in Bristol against what he regarded as the abuses in the Church such as the veneration of the Virgin, images, relics, pilgrimages, the worship of the saints and other features of Church life created enormous controversy and uproar in the town. Several preachers immediately sprang to the defence of the established order in the Church, most notably William Hubberdyne who was almost as popular a preacher as Latimer. The clash of rival pulpit orators created enough uproar and disturbance for the matter to be brought to the attention of Thomas Cromwell. As the king's chief minister, Cromwell was concerned above all else with upholding the royal authority and maintaining public order; he appointed a Commission to investigate the matter which reported on the 'infamy, discord, strife and debate' which had been stirred up in Bristol. How far it all affected the opinions of the majority of the people in Bristol it is impossible to say; probably very little, for during all the religious changes of the next few years there were few in the town who were prepared to defy the royal authority by actively or publicly supporting either cause. But it was against this background of bitter controversy and theological argument in Bristol that the first steps were taken during the 1530s which were to lead to the dismantling of the ecclesiastical edifice which only a few years earlier had seemed to be totally secure.

Another popular conservative preacher who responded to Latimer's sermons was Roger Edgeworth, a staunch Catholic who was a frequent visitor to Bristol. In his Bristol sermons Edgeworth attacked the 'heretics that soweth cockle and ill seeds among the corn, settyng forth sectes and divisions'. Edgeworth also claimed that theological disputes, the spread of Protestant views and time spent by the laity in studying and debating upon the meaning of Scripture would destroy the vital commercial and trading life of Bristol.

> "I have known manye in this towne, that studienge divinitie, hath killed a merchant, and some of other occupations by their busy labours in the Scriptures, hath shut up the shoppe windowes."

Edgeworth was in no doubt that the basis of Bristol's wealth lay in trade beyond the seas, and that if this should cease or if the enterprise of merchants and the courage of sailors should fail then the prosperity of Bristol was doomed.

> ". . . if for one storme or twayne, or one loss or twayne, he should abhorre and give off going to the sea, there would at the last no man aventure to the seas, and then farewell this citye of Bristowe."

Preachers such as Latimer, Hubberdyne and Edgeworth were followed to Bristol by numerous others, representing every shade of religious opinion in the country from extreme reformers to the staunchest supporters of the existing order in the Church, so that in Bristol, more than in any other town in England, all the various upheavals and changes of the Reformation were accompanied by violent exchanges from rival pulpits in the parish churches of the town.

One aspect of the Reformation which had a profound effect in Bristol was the dissolution of the monasteries, friaries, chantries and other religious foundations of which there were many in and around the town. As part of the long process of the dissolution of the religious houses, masterminded from London by Thomas Cromwell, Bristol was visited by numerous Commissioners collecting evidence about finances, lands and property, or about the conduct and behaviour of the monks, friars and nuns, or enquiring into the state of the religious houses, and eventually taking control of all the monastic wealth and property in the name of the King. Among the most cynical of all the Commissioners was a priest, Richard Layton, who had a very low opinion of the religious houses and their inmates and a total contempt for some of the contemporary abuses in the Church. In 1535 Layton wrote amusingly to Cromwell from Bristol describing the monasteries he had visited and some of the relics he had collected in Wiltshire and Somerset.

"Please it your mastership to understand, that yesternight late we came from Glastonburie to Bristow to Saint Austin's, where we begin this morning, intending this day to dispatche bothe this howse here, beinge but xiiii canons, and also the Gauntes where there be iiii or v. By this bringer, my servant, I sende yowe reliques, first two flowers wrapped in white and blacke sarcenet that on Christmas eve *hora ipsa qua Christus natus fuerat* will spring, burgen and bere blossoms . . . Ye shall also receive a bage of reliques, wherein ye shall see strange thinges . . . as Gode's cote, our Ladie's smock, parte of Gode's supper . . . *Pars petre super qua natus erat Jesus in Bethlehem,* belyke ther is in Bethlehem plentie of stones and some quarrie and maketh ther mangers of stone. The scripture of every thing shall declare you all; and all these of Maiden Bradley, where is an holy Father prior, and hath but vi children, and but one daughter married yet of the goodes of the monasterie, trusting shortly to marry the reste. His sonnes be tall men waiting upon him, and he thankes Gode he never meddled with married women, but all with maidens the fairest coulde be gottyn, and always married them right well. The Pope, considering his fragilitie, gave hym licence to keep a whore . . .

I have crosses of silver and golde, some which I sende you not now because I have more that shall be delivered me this night by the prior of Maiden Bradley himself . . . and perchaunce I shall fynde some thyng here . . .

At Bruton and Glastonburie ther is nothing notable; the brethren be so straite kept that they cannot offende, but faine they woulde if they mighte, as they confesse, and so the fault is not in them.

From Sainte Austin's withoute Bristowe, this Saint

35

Bartholomew's day,* at iiii of the cloke in the morning, by the spedy hand of your moste assured poor prieste, Richard Layton"

Between 1536 and 1539 all the monastic houses and all their lands and property passed into the King's hands. St Augustine's, the richest of all the Bristol monastic houses, with lands and property which brought it an annual income of £692 2s. 7d, surrendered to the King on December 9th 1539. The anonymous chroniclers who continued Ricart's *Kalendar* described part of these far-reaching changes as follows:

"1539

Memorandum, that this yere all the Friars of this Towne surrendered their places unto the Kinge's most high majestie's hands.

1540

Memorandum, that this yere the Abbott and Convent of Seynt Augustynes of Bristowe surrendered that monastry unto the kynge's moost noble graces hands. And so in like wise the maister and his brothers of Gauntes, with their assents made. Memorandum, That this yere the scite and the demeanes of the Gauntes of Bristowe, then dissolved, with all manors, landes, tenementes, and other the hereditaments belonging to the same, were purchased by the Mayor and Cominaltie of Bristowe abovementioned of the kynges highnes, for the summe of £1,000 . . ."

The former abbey of St Augustine was made into the cathedral of the newly-created diocese of Bristol in 1542, and part of the former abbey buildings became the bishop's palace.

More royal commissioners visited Bristol during the further religious changes of the reign of Edward VI (1547-53), when sweeping reforms were ordered to be made in the services and furnishings of the parish churches, and when the greater part of the large store of possessions of gold and silver belonging to the Bristol parish churches was confiscated by the Crown officials. Religious controversy continued to affect Bristol throughout the reign of Queen Mary (1553-58), when Catholicism was restored, and when several Bristolians were burnt at the stake for their refusal to conform to the established religion as decreed by the Queen. The

* i.e. August 24 1535

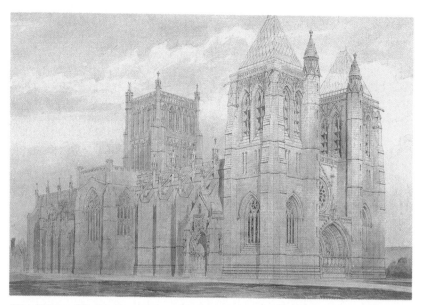

The Abbey of St Augustine became Bristol Cathedral in 1542 and in its truncated form attracted little favourable comment from visitors. The architect's drawing shows the new nave and western towers welded on to the existing building in the late 19th century.

names of five of those who were burnt are recorded on a memorial in Highbury Chapel on St Michael's Hill, near the spot where their horrific executions took place. Early in Queen Mary's reign the Catholic preacher, Roger Edgeworth, again visited Bristol, and rebuked the citizens for their refusal to accept the restored Catholic faith and for their continuing controversies over religion.

"Here among you in this citie some will hear masse, some will heare none by theyr good wills, some will be shriven, some will not, but for feare, or else for shame, some will pay tithes and offerings, some will not, . . . some will pray for the dead, some will not. I heare of muche suche dissension among you."

Those who stubbornly and steadfastly refused to conform to the Catholic faith in spite of all persuasion, were tried for heresy before Dr William Dalby, the vicar-general of the diocese, and if found guilty and all threats failed, they were sentenced to be burnt. A vivid account of one such execution on St Michael's Hill is given by the famous Elizabethan author and martyrologist, John Foxe, in *Acts and Monuments* first published in 1563 and better known as

Foxe's *Book of Martyrs*. Foxe, who seems from the detail he gives to have obtained the account from an eye-witness, describes the execution by burning of a Bristol weaver, William Saxton, on September 18th 1556. He was condemned for denying that the flesh and blood of Christ were present in the Mass, and for affirming that the Holy Eucharist was not the true body of Christ but material bread only.

"The eighth day of August (1556) was brought William Saxton (or Sarton), weaver of Bristol, before one Dalby chancellor of Bristol aforesaid; and by him committed to prison, and also condemned for holding that the sacrament was a sign of a holy thing: also he denied, that the flesh and blood of Christ is there after their words of consecration. He was burnt the 18th day of September, anno 1556, and as he went to the fire, he sung psalms. The sheriff, John Griffith, had prepared green wood to burn him; but one master John Pikes, pitying the man, caused divers to go with him to Ridland (Redland), half a mile off, who brought good store of helme-sheaves, which indeed made good dispatch with little pain, in comparison to that he should have suffered with the green wood. In the mean space, whilst they went for the sheaves, the said Saxton made many good exhortations to the people, and after died constantly and patiently with great joyfulness."[3]

Perhaps the most famous visitor to Bristol during the sixteenth century, and certainly the one who was received with the greatest acclaim and lavish civic welcome, was Queen Elizabeth who spent a week in the city during August 1574, and was magnificently entertained by the Corporation. Elaborate and expensive preparations were made to receive the Queen, including newly decorating the High Cross and the city gates, sanding the streets, and providing elaborate pageants, speeches of welcome and entertainments for the Queen and her Court. The Queen was accommodated in the recently-built Great House on St Augustine's Back, near the site of the present Colston Hall; the house belonged to Mr John Young who was later knighted by the Queen for his hospitality. Ricart's *Kalendar* described the visit in the following terms:

"1574

This yere on Satterday, beinge the xiii day of August, the Queene came to this citie, and Mr Mayor and the Common Counsell ridinge with foote clothes, receaved her highnes within Laffardes gate. And ther Mr Mayor delyvered the gilt Mace unto her Majestie, and she then presentlie delyvered it to him againe. And so Mr Mayor knelinge whiles Mr John Popham esqier, Recorder of this citie, made an Oracon, did after it was ended stand up, and delyvered a faire purse wrought with silke and golde having an hundred poundes in golde in it, unto her highnes. And thereupon Mr Mayor and his brethren toke theire horses, and Mr Mayor rode nighe before the Queen betweene two Sergantes-at-armes. And the residewe of the Common Counsell rode next afore the Nobilitie and Trumpeters, and so passed throughe the towne unto Mr John Yonges howse, where she lay untill Satterday then next followinge . . . And duringe her abode here (amonge other thinges devised for plesure) there weare 400 soldiers in one sute of apparell, whereof 300 weare harquebussiers and 100 pikemen in corselettes. Also there was made a greate large forte standinge in Trenemill meade over againste Gibtaylor, which was assaulted by land and water 3 daies. And there was also another litle forte called the base fortt, standinge upon the hill beyond, which was wonne the first night that the assault was given. And the Queene was there at every assault duringe the saide three daies, for whose standinge there was builded a large scaffolde of tymber in the Marshe. Whiche martiall experiment beinge very costlie and chargeable (especially in gonnepowder), the Queene and Nobilitie liked verie well of, and gave Mr Mayor and his brethren greate thankes for theire doinges."[4]

It was during Queen Elizabeth's visit to Bristol in 1574 that she is reputed to have made her well-known remark about St Mary Redcliffe that it was 'the fairest, goodliest, and most famous parish church in England', a comment which she might well have made, although there is no contemporary evidence for it.

Visitors of a more humble kind arrived in Bristol in 1577. They were Eskimos, who were brought to Bristol by Martin Frobisher after yet another voyage from Bristol to North America in a fruitless search for a north-west passage to the East. Frobisher also brought some ore which was thought to be gold and of which high hopes were for a time entertained; but the ore proved to be worthless, and the unfortunate Eskimos soon died, unable to withstand either the climate or the infectious diseases of Bristol, though not before they had provided an unusual spectacle and entertainment for the citizens. William Adam's *Chronicle of Bristol* compiled a few years later, describes the incident as follows:

"Captaine Frobisher in a ship of our Queene's of the burden of 200 tons, came into Kingrode from Cathay; who brought certain ore from thence, which was esteemed to be very rich and full of gold; it was heavy, and so hard that it would strike fire like flint; some of it was tried in our castle, and the rest sent to London, where it was esteemed not worth the charges in refining. They brought likewise a man called Callicho, and a woman called Ignorth: they were savage people and fed only upon raw flesh. The ninth of October he rowed in a little boat made of skin in the water at the Backe, where he killed two ducks with a dart, and when he had done carried his boat through the marsh upon his back; the like he did at the weir and other places where many beheld him. He would hit a duck a good distance off and not miss. They died here within a month."[5]

Finally, we have a description of Bristol in the late sixteenth century by William Camden, the most famous of Elizabethan topographical writers and an acute observer of the towns, ports, villages, industries and, above all, of the antiquities of the realm. Camden commented on the fine situation of Bristol and its population which he thought ranked it next in size after London and York. He was impressed by the sewers which made the city very clean in great contrast to most Elizabethan towns.

"The sewers (which they call *Goutes*) are so contrived to carry off and wash away the filth, that nothing is wanting that can conduce to cleanliness or health."

This is in marked contrast to early nineteenth century descriptions of Bristol which, as will be shown in Chapter 5, reveal inadequate drains, poor water supply and appalling filth everywhere.

Camden commented also upon the fine harbour, 'which admits ships under sail into the heart of the city', and which brought great trade. 'The citizens carry on a profitable trade all over Europe, and send ships to the most distant parts of America.' He remarked upon

Opposite: In contrast to the Cathedral, St Mary Redcliffe often attracted much attention.

the hospitals or almshouses, and naturally, the large number of fine parish churches in and around the city.

"Hospitals are also every where erected for the benefit of the poor, and, churches to the glory of God. Among the fairest of the latter is St Mary de Radcliffe, without the walls, with a grand ascent of steps, the whole so spacious and well built, with an arched roof of stone and a lofty steeple, as to exceed, in my opinion, all the parish churches of England that I have yet seen . . .

Near this is another church called Temple, whose tower shakes so when the bells ring, that it has parted from the rest of the building, and left a chink from top to bottom three fingers broad, opening and closing as the bells ring. Nor must we forget St Stephen's church, whose lofty tower was built at great expence and in a beautiful style by one Shipward, citizen and merchant in the last age."[6]

Notes
1. E G R Taylor (ed.), A Brief Summe of Geographie by Roger Barlow, *Hakluyt Society,* Second Series, LXIX, 1931-2, 47, 179-80.
2. L T Smith (ed.), *The Itinerary of John Leland 1535-43,* V, 1910, 86-93.
3. G Townsend (ed.), *John Foxe's Acts and Monuments,* 1843-9, VIII, 251, 503-4, 737.
4. L T Smith (ed.), Ricart's Kalendar, *Camden Society,* New Series, V, 1872.
5. F Fox (ed.), *Adam's Chronicle of Bristol,* 1910.
6. R Gough (ed.), *William Camden's Britannia 1586,* 1, 1806, 86-7, 122-7.

Other Sources
T Wright (ed.), Letters relating to the Suppression of the Monasteries, *Camden Society,* XXVI, 1843, 7-10, 58-9.
V Stefansson (ed.), *The Three Voyages of Martin Frobisher,* 11, 1938, 237-8.
J Latimer, *Sixteenth Century Bristol,* 1908.
C M MacInnes, *Bristol: A Gateway of Empire,* 1968.
M D Lobel and E M Carus Wilson, *Historic Towns - Bristol,* 1975.
K G Powell, *The Marian Martyrs and the Reformation in Bristol,* Bristol Historical Association, 1972.
J H Bettey, *Bristol Parish Churches during the Reformation,* Bristol Historical Association, 1979.
G R Elton, *Policy and Police,* 1972, 112-20.
J H Bettey, *Church and Community in Bristol during the Sixteenth Century,* Bristol Record Society, 1983.
J Vanes, *The Port of Bristol in the Sixteenth Century,* Bristol Historical Association, 1977.
P McGrath (ed.), A Bristol Miscellany, *Bristol Record Society,* XXXVII, 1985.

THREE

SEVENTEENTH CENTURY VISITS
'The City is Sweet and Cleane'

From the early seventeenth century onwards the number of visitors who left an account of their impressions of Bristol increased rapidly, and the problem of selecting a representative collection becomes more difficult. Travel became easier and safer in spite of the fact that many roads remained in a very bad condition, especially in winter; cartography improved, more accurate maps of the country become available, and interest in travel and in topographical writing grew steadily.

In spite of its importance as a regional capital and as a flourishing port having busy trading links with France, Spain, Ireland, and increasingly with the New World, Bristol remained throughout the seventeenth century very small by modern standards. Its population on the eve of the Civil War in 1642 was no more than 15,000 and most of the town was still crammed within its medieval walls; by the end of the century the population had still not reached 20,000. Nonetheless visitors were greatly impressed with the city, by its situation, by the crowded shipping along the banks of the Avon and Frome, by the fine churches and public buildings, including Bristol bridge—lined on either side by shops and houses and which until the Civil War was surmounted by the medieval Chapel of the Assumption, built over and across the thoroughfare of the bridge, a superbly beautiful 14th century building with a great tower over 100 feet high which must have presented a remarkable and dramatic landmark in the centre of the town. Visitors were also struck by the industries, trade and evident wealth of the city and by the numerous merchants with their opulent houses all still crowded into the medieval heart of the city.

Among the most informative descriptions is that produced by three soldiers, a Captain, a Lieutenant and an 'Ancient' or Ensign. They came from Norwich and journeyed through England in the summer of 1634, noting all the places which they visited. Little is known of the three soldiers, but the actual writer appears to have been the Lieutenant whose name was Hammond. The soldiers evidently enjoyed their visit to Bristol, and extolled its shipping and busy harbour, the cleanliness of the city and its fine public buildings, and the splendour of the Avon gorge. As soldiers they were also interested in the defence of the city, and in the military exercises of the Trained Bands consisting of three companies of foot soldiers. Their description of Bristol in 1634, with the punctuation and some of the spelling modernised, was as follows:

"This Citty stands sweetly in a pleasant Cock-pit valley, yet with an ascent to the heart thereof where stands a fayre Crosse in the midst betweene both Bridges, lately and richly beautify'd, and not much inferior to that in Coventry. To it comes 4 large and fayre streets from the 4 chiefe quarters of the City, viz. High Street which is the fayrest from the great Bridge in Somersetshire; Broad Street from the Key Bridge in Gloucestershire; Wine Street from the Castle; and Corne Street from the Marsh.

This parcell of ground the Marsh, is a very pleasant and delighfull place, and with as much Art added thereto as can conveniently bee both for walkes, a Bowling ground, and other

Wine Street, in the 17th century, was the thoroughfare between the Castle and City Cross. The entrance to the Guard-house is just visible.

44

recreations for the rich Marchants and gentile Citizens, adorned with many fayre Trees, wherein constantly the City Captaines drill and muster and exercise the City Forces; neere 3 partes thereof is surrounded by the River which divides itself from the maine streame att the very point of the Marsh, which causeth a sweet and pleasant Eccho of their martiall Musicke, Drums, Fifes, and volleys of Shot; the one arme whereof (i.e. the Frome) runneth downe betwixt that and the Minster of Gloucestershire, which is the principall quay and wharfe, where all their fayre and rich Shipping lye, even to that Bridge. The other Streame (i.e. the Avon) runs through the city next Somersetshire down to Bath, over which is built a fayre stone arch't Bridge with hansome neat Houses and Ships on either side thereof like a Street which may for its length compare with London.

The City is very sweet and cleane in respect of the quotidian tydes that wash and cleanse her lower parts, and the vaults and sewers that are under all, or most the channells of her upper parts. In her wee found (besides that fayre and strong Fabricke of the Cathedrall which was newly finished) 18 Churches which are all fayrely beautify'd, richly adorn'd and sweetly kept, and in the major part of them are neat, rich and melodious Organs that are constantly played on. Their Pulpitts are most curious in which the Citizens have spared no cost nor forwardnesse to beautify and adorne (a pious and religious example for all our kingdom) . . .

For her Marchants, they are rich and numerous, using Traffique to most parts of Christendome; they have a commodious Custome House, and a kind of Exchange, where they constantly meet every day . . .

For her Buildings, especially the Churches, they are most strong and Sumptuous."

Lieutenant Hammond went on to describe the government of Bristol, with its Mayor and Corporation, the merchants' halls, the Trained Bands who exercised for the defence of the city, and the churches, especially the Cathedral and St Mary Redcliffe. Bristol castle the soldiers found in great decay and almost ruinous. Down the Avon they visited St Vincent's rock and the Hot Wells where they found a large company who came to wash in the water as well as to drink it. Finally, after taking 'a cup of Bristow Milke', the three soldiers left on the next stage of their journey which took them over the top of Mendip to Wells.

A similar account of Bristol was given by another traveller, a Cornishman called Peter Mundy who came to the city in 1639. Mundy was born in the Cornish port of Penryn in about 1596; he had spent his life in travel and had made trading journeys to Constantinople, India, Japan, Russia and many other places, keeping a careful account of all that he saw. In 1639 he returned to Cornwall, but his restless spirit did not long allow him to stay there and he made a 'petty progresse' in England and Wales. Mundy was greatly attracted by Bristol, and even thought of settling in the city, being almost persuaded

"through the Commodiousnesse, plenty, and pleasantnesse of the place to have taken uppe my habitation here; but I had a Mind to see Farther first."

Like other seventeenth century visitors to Bristol, Peter Mundy commented upon the situation and trade of the port, the ships, and the cleanliness of the city. He also noted that most of the houses had vaults or cellars, and that for this reason they used horse-drawn sledges rather than carts in the streets, so as not to damage the vaults. He also saw the famous Bristol 'nails'

"By the High Crosse is the Exchange where are many curious and costly pillars of brasse, about 3 or 4 foote high, broad at the foote and toppe, sett off purpose for men to leane on, pay and tell money, etc."

Mundy was also fascinated to see that in many Bristol houses dogs were employed at working a wheel which turned the spit before the fire on which meat was cooked.

". . . scarce a house that hath nott a dogge to turne the spitt in a little wooden wheele."

His overall impression of the city was

"Bristol is even a little London for Merchants, shipping, and great, well-furnished markets etc., and I think second to it in the kingdom of England."[1]

During the Civil War of the 1640s Bristol was a key stronghold and of great strategic importance to both sides in the conflict. As a flourishing port, protected by its rivers and walls, with a strongly-fortified castle, Bristol played an important part in the War, and many prominent men, both royalists and parliamentarians, came to the city, although few had time to record their impressions in any detail. Its strategic importance was emphasised by the notable puritan preacher and parliamentarian William Prynne who wrote that

> "the whole kingdom looked upon Bristol as a place of the greatest consequence of any in England, next to London, as the metropolis, key, magazine of the West . . .,"[2]

while the royalist Earl of Clarendon described Bristol as

> "a great, rich and populous city . . . easily able to give the law to Somerset and Gloucestershire."[3]

In July 1643 the city was taken by the royalist forces under the command of Prince Rupert and Sir Ralph Hopton, and King Charles himself came to Bristol to congratulate his forces on the capture of England's second city, with all its wealth and shipping, which had provided a great encouragement to the royalist cause. During his visit the King stayed in an house in Small Street. The royalists occupied Bristol for over two years; Queen Henrietta Maria visited the city in April 1644, and in March 1645 the King's eldest son, the young Prince Charles, then fourteen years of age, set up his headquarters in Bristol Castle, as nominal General of the West.

In August, with the royalist cause suffering reverses all over the country, Prince Rupert once more took command in Bristol and, although cut off from all other royalist forces, attempted to defend the city from the advancing parliamentarians. The attack came at 1.00am on the morning of September 10th 1645, when the parliamentary army led by Sir Thomas Fairfax and Oliver Cromwell launched an assault. Faced with greatly superior forces, and fearing lest the city should be completely destroyed in the conflict, Prince Rupert decided, after some hours of fighting, to surrender. He was granted reasonable terms by Fairfax, and the next day, September 11th 1645, the Prince marched his defeated forces out from his headquarters in the Royal Fort. A contemporary newsletter recorded that

> "The Prince was clad in scarlet, very richly laid in silver lace, mounted upon a very gallant black Barbary horse; the General and the Prince rode together, the General giving the Prince the right hand all the way."[4]

The loss of Bristol proved to be a decisive blow for the King's cause, and the King himself reacted with an angry protest to his nephew Prince Rupert, accusing him of having needlessly surrendered the city.

Nephew,

Though the loss of Bristoll be a blow to me, yet your surrendering it as you did is of so much affliction to me, that it
makes me forget not only the consideration of that place, but is
likewise the greatest trial of my constancy that hath yet
befallen me; for what is to be done after one that is so near me
as you are, both in blood and friendship, submits himself to so
mean an action (I give it the easiest term) I have so much to
say that I will say no more of it: only, lest rashness of
judgement be laid to my charge, I must remember one of your
letters of the 12 Aug., whereby you assured me, (that if no
mutiny happened), you would keep Bristoll four months. Did
you keep it for four days? Was there anything like a Mutiny?
More questions might be asked, but now, I confess, to so little
purpose. My conclusion is, to desire you to seek your
subsistence (until it shall please God to determine my
condition) somewhere beyond the seas, to which end I send you
herewith a pass; and I pray God to make you sensible of your
present condition, and give you means to redeem what you
have lost; for I shall have no greater joy in a victory, than a
just occasion without blushing to assure of my being

Your loving oncle and most

faithful friend.

With the letter and the pass the King sent a revocation of all
Rupert's commands and commissions.

The parliamentarians were, naturally, elated at the capture of
such an important and strategic stronghold, the last seaport
remaining in royalist hands, and on September 14th, 1645 Oliver
Cromwell wrote from Bristol to William Lenthall, Speaker of the
House of Commons a long letter describing in detail the capture of
Bristol, and concluding

"Thus I have given you a true, but not full account of this
great business; wherein he that runs may read, that all this is
none other than the work of God. He must be a very Atheist
that doth not acknowledge it . . . Sir, they that have been
employed in this service know that faith and prayer obtained
this city for you. I do not say ours only, but of the people of
God with you and all England over, who have wrestled with
God for a blessing in this very thing . . ."[5]

Oliver Cromwell, from a miniature by Cooper.

In September 1651 another royal visitor passed briefly through Bristol; this was King Charles II, a hunted fugitive fleeing in disguise from Cromwell's army after the crushing defeat of the royalist's attempt to seize power in the battle of Worcester. Charles, disguised as a servant, hoped to find a ship in Bristol to take him to safety abroad. Failing in his purpose, the King with his loyal friend and protectress, Jane Lane, sought temporary refuge with the Norton family in their manor house at Abbots Leigh, while the parliamentary army scoured the country in search of him. After a few days in hiding, the King was able to continue his secret flight to the south coast where he eventually, and after several narrow escapes, found a ship to take him to France.

During the period of the Commonwealth, John Evelyn the diarist visited Bristol in the summer of 1654, and recorded his impressions of the busy town and port with its fine buildings, although the Castle which had played an important part in the Civil War had already been 'slighted' and virtually destroyed. Evelyn also commented on the trade between Bristol and the New World, and on the sugar refineries which in 1654 were already important in the manufacturing industry of Bristol; above all he was impressed by the sight of the towering cliffs of the Avon gorge.

". . . Bristol, a city emulating London, not for its large extent, but manner of buildings, shops, bridge, Traffique, Exchange, Marketplace, etc. The Governor shew'd us the Castle, of no great concernment. The City wholy Mercantile, as standing near the famous Severne, commodiously for Ireland and the Western world. Here I first saw the manner of refining suggar and casting it into loaves, where we had a collation of Eggs fried in the suggar furnace, together with excellent Spanish wine; but what I saw was most stupendous to me, was the rock of St Vincent, a little distance from the Towne, the precipe whereoff is equal to any thing of that nature I have seene in the most confragose cataracts of the Alpes, the river gliding betweene them after an extraordinary depth. Here we went searching for Diamonds, and to the Hot Well of water at its foote".[6]

In 1662 the famous Anglican divine and scholar, Thomas Fuller, published his celebrated work, *The Worthies of England.* This not only gives information about notable persons, but also described the character, produce, manufactures and buildings of each part of

England. Fuller knew Bristol well, since from 1634 to 1641 he had been rector of Broadwindsor in Dorset which at that time was in the diocese of Bristol, and he had represented Bristol in the convocation of Canterbury in 1640. In his book he commented upon the remarkable cleanliness of the streets of Bristol, and on the sledges which were used in the streets instead of carts, on Bristol bridge with the houses on either side which 'counterfeiteth a continued street', and on the fine houses of the rich merchants. Fuller also commented upon the splendour of St Mary Redcliffe which he thought should have been the cathedral.

> "Redcliffe church in this city clearly carrieth away the credit from all parish churches in England . . . most stately the ascent thereunto by many stairs, which at the last plentifully recompenseth their pains who climb them up, with the magnificent structure both without and within."

Fuller noted the importance of the soap-making trade in Bristol, and the water from St Vincent's rock, 'sovereign for sores and sicknesses; to be washed in, or drunk of, to be either outwardly or inwardly applied'. Like other visitors, he enjoyed the famous Bristol 'milk' or sherry. Above all, he paid tribute to the important part which Bristol and Bristol merchants had played in the discovery and exploration of the New World.

> "No city in England (London alone excepted) hath, in so short a time, bred more brave and bold seamen, advantaged for western voyages by its situation. They have not only been merchants, but adventurers, possessed, with a public spirit for the general good; aiming not so much to return wealthier as wiser; not always to enrich themselves as inform posterity by their discoveries. Of these, some have been but merely casual; when going to fish for cod they have found a country, or some eminent bay, river, or haven of importance, unknown before. Others were intentional, wherein they have sown experiments, with great pains, cost and danger, that ensuing ages may freely reap benefit thereof."[7]

Another visitor to Bristol who was greatly struck by the size, trade and prosperity of the city, and by the great pride of Bristolians in their fine city, was Marmaduke Rawdon, a merchant of York, who visited Bristol in 1665. His account of his impressions of the city was as follows:

> "This is a cittie well populated, of greate trade, hath a

51

cathedrall, but I thinke the meanest in England; they have convenient havens for ships; they imitate London very much in their hospitall boyes in blew coates, which waites uppon the mayor to church, their liveries in their companies, and severall other thinges; itt hath its exchange, where are severall brasse pillars about an ell high for people to leane uppon, and to talke, tell money, signe anie writinges, or the like. In this cittie are many proper men but very few handsome women, and most of them ill bred, being generally men and women very proud, nott affable to strangers, but rather much admiring themselves, soe that an ordinary fellow that is but a freeman of Bristol, he conceits himselfe to be as grave as a senator of Rome, and very sparinge of his hatt, in soe much that their preachers hath told them of it in the pupitt.

They use in the cittie most sleds to carry their goods, and the drivers such rude people, that they will have their horses uppon a strangers backe before they be aware. Here was a castle built large and strong by Robert Earle of Gloucester, base son of King Henry the First, but in these late warres demolisht and made dwelling houses of. As you goe down the river Avon, a mile from the towne is a well covered every tyde with salt water, yett the water is very freshe; itt is called the hott well, and is constantly as warme as bloode; itt hath several medicinall virtues.

Above itt are some rocks of reddish earth and stones which they call St Vincent's rocke, where within the earth, about 8 inches deepe, are found those stones they call Bristol diamonds, which are very bright and naturally pointed with squares, as if they were cutt on purpose. On the other side of the river is an extraordinary cold spring, where the ships water for their voyages; three miles below the river, att a small towne called Pill, rideth the great ships. The river is very windinge, having high hills with trees of each side, very pleasant to behold, and a man would wonder how the river found his passage amongst soe many high rocks. They have uppon one of their gates the picture of Brenus and Belinus who they would fancie to be the founders of their cittie, but by the best writers itt began to peepe out a little before William the Conqueror. They have one church, called Ratcliffe Church, which excells the cathedrall, and was built by one William Cannings, a rich

Block of houses in King Street built in 1664. The Llandoger Tavern originally occupied only the house farthest from the river. The two houses nearest the river were lost during the Blitz.

marchant, who was five times mayor of Bristol; he built another church at Westbury, two miles from thence, did furnish itt with canons and, taking orders, was Dean thereof himselfe. He maintained for the space of eight yeares 800 handicraft men, besides carpenters and masons, and maintained 2470 ton of shippinge for Kinge Edward the 4th; with which I will take leave of Bristol.''

One of the most famous as well as informative visitors to Bristol during the seventeenth century was the diarist Samuel Pepys who came to the city on June 13th 1668. Pepys held the very important position of Secretary of the Admiralty; in June 1668 he took a short holiday and journeyed with his wife, Elizabeth, and her maid, Deborah Willet, first to Oxford and from there via Hungerford to Salisbury and thence to Bath. From Bath the party travelled to Bristol to spend the day there.

The whole journey illustrates very well the problems which faced seventeenth century travellers, the bad roads, expensive and inadeqate inns, the absence of sign-posts and the difficulty of finding the way especially across open country like Salisbury Plain or the Berkshire Downs where the correct route was often uncertain and where there were few landmarks. It was frequently necessary for Pepys to hire expensive guides to show the party the road, at Salisbury he was indignant at the exorbitant prices he was charged at the inn and for horse-hire, while at Bath they found 'our beds good but we lousy'. Even with a guide the party got lost on the way across Salisbury Plain between Wilton and Bath, and only by great good fortune did they manage to arrive at Chitterne and found an hospitable inn just before darkness fell; otherwise they would have had to spend the night on the Plain. As it was the only room at the inn was occupied by a pedlar, but the unfortunate fellow was immediately turned out of bed so that Pepys and his party could be accommodated. Likewise on their return journey to London they completely lost their way in the Kennet valley between Newbury and Reading.

One reason for visiting Bristol was that the maid, Deborah Willet, had been brought up there and some members of her family still lived in the city, including her uncle, William Butts, who was a substantial Bristol merchant. The party was received with tremendous pleasure and enthusiasm by Deborah's family and friends, while Pepys himself as an eminent and influential Admiralty official was treated with great deference by the Bristol merchants and ship-owners. The whole visit to Bristol, vividly described by Pepys in his *Diary* with his customary enthusiasm and intense interest in all that he saw, was an idyllic episode in their holiday.

A coach was hired to take the party from Bath to Bristol, and even in June the roads were bad so that the journey took over three hours. In Bristol Pepys first visited a barber to be shaved, and then walked with his wife through the city which he described in his *Diary* as

> ". . . in every respect another London that one can hardly know it to stand in the country . . . No carts, it standing generally on vaults, only dog carts."

The maid, Deborah Willet, went to visit her uncle and family while Pepys, with his detailed professional interest in ships and shipping, went to the quay 'a most large and noble place'. There he found a warship being built for the Admiralty, the *Edgar* which was almost completed in the yard of the Bristol shipbuilder, Francis Bailey. The party were then invited to dine with Deborah Willet's uncle, and the rest of Pepys' delightful account of their entertainment in Bristol, together with his note of the expenditure for the day is worth quoting in full from his *Diary*:

"Walked back to the *Sun* where I will find Deb come back and with her her uncle a sober merchant very good company and is so like one of our sober wealthy London merchants as pleased me mightily. Here dined and much good talk with him

—   7s — 6d

Then walked with him and my wife and company to round the key and to the ship and he showed me the Custom House and made me understand many things of the place and led us through Marsh street where our girl was born but Lord the joy that was among the old poor people of the place to see Mrs. Willets daughter it seems her mother being a brave woman and mightily beloved. And so brought us a back way by surprize to his house where a substantial good house and well furnished and did give us good entertainment of strawberries a whole venison pasty cold and plenty of brave wine and above all Bristoll milk. Where comes in another poor woman who hearing that Deb was here did come running hither and with her eyes so full of joy that she could not speak when she came in that it made me weep too I protest that I was not able to speak to her which I would have done to divert her tears. His wife a good woman and so sober and substantial as I was never more pleased anywhere.

Servant maid   —   2s — 0d

So thence took leave and he with us through the city where in walking I find the city pay him great respect and he the like to the meanest which pleased me mightily. He showed us the place where the merchants meet here and a fine cross yet standing like Cheapside. And so to the *Horse Shoe* where paying the reckoning   —   2s — 6d

We back by moonshine to the Bath again about 10 a'clock bad way and giving the coachman   —   1s —0d
went all of us to bed."[8]

In 1671 we can obtain our first really detailed view of Bristol, its topography, streets, quays, buildings and open spaces in the splendid perspective plan of the city published by a Bristol mercer,

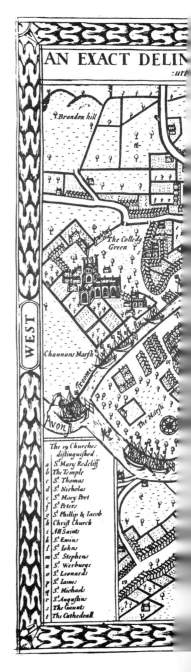

Brandon hill

The Colledg Green

WEST

Channans Marsh

Froome

Avon

The Marsh

The 19 Churches
distinguished.
a | S.t Mary Redcliff
b | The Temple
c | S.t Thomas
d | S.t Nicholas
e | S.t Mary Port
f | S.t Peters
g | S.t Phillip & Iacob
h | Chrift Church
i | All Saints
k | S.t Ewins
l | S.t Iohns
m | S.t Stephens
n | S.t Werburge
o | S.t Leonards
p | S.t Iames
q | S.t Michaels
r | S.t Augustins
s | The Gaunts
t | The Cathedrall

Millerd's Map of 1671, with the castle now demolished. The rapid expansion of the city was about to begin.

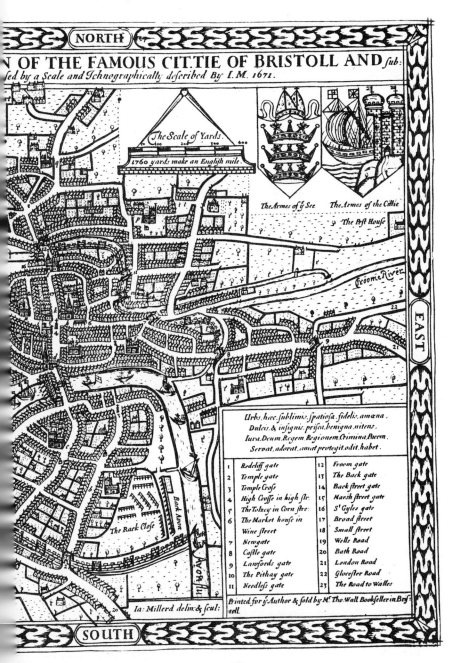

James or Jacob Millerd and entitled *An Exact Delineation of the Famous Cittie of Bristol and Suburbs Thereof.* Although a mercer by trade, Millerd possessed great ability as a surveyor and cartographer, and the map of 1671 provides a remarkably clear and detailed picture of Bristol. The value of Millerd's work was soon recognised, for the City Council ordered that he should be officially thanked and granted him a silver tankard valued at £10, while the Society of Merchant Venturers voted him a piece of plate worth £5 in recognition of his work.

During the course of the seventeenth century the population of Bristol more than doubled. At the beginning of the century the population was probably not much more than 12,000, while by 1700 the city had grown to be the second largest in the kingdom with a population of over 20,000 people. One consequence of this was a rapid expansion of the suburbs, as the city spread beyond the ancient limits of its walls. In his plan of Bristol of 1671 James Millerd remarked on the spread of houses and noted that

".. . in few years past, this Cittie hath been much augmented by the increase of buildings in most parts thereof, especially on the West and North-West sides, where the rising of the Hill St Michael being converted into Comely buildings and pleasant gardens makes a very beautiful addition to the suburbs thereof."

The later editions of Millerd's plan of the city dating from 1684 and 1696 show the rapid expansion of the suburbs during the later seventeenth century. After the Civil War more space became available inside the city walls with the demolition of Bristol castle in 1655 and the erection of shops and houses on much of the site. Millerd commented in 1673 that 'since the late Warrs (it) hath bin demolished and is now turned into faire streets and pleasant dwellings . . .'

During the later seventeenth century Roger North who was the Recorder of Bristol wrote a biography of his brother Francis North, Lord Guildford, and included a brief but extremely interesting description of Bristol, in which he emphasizes the importance of the trade of the city, especially with America and the West Indies, and also remarks on the wealth and pride of the prosperous Bristol merchants. He also alludes to the growing traffic in slaves which was to form such an important aspect of Bristol's trade during the eighteenth century.

". . . Bristol, which is a maritime trading city, with a small cathedral. It is remarkable there, that all men that are dealers, even in shop trades, launch into adventures by sea, chiefly to the West India plantations and Spain. A poor shopkeeper, that sells candles, will have a bale of stockings, or a piece of stuff for Nevis or Virginia etc., and rather than fail, they trade in men . . .

Christenings and burials pompous and beyond imagination. A man who dies worth three hundred pounds, will order two hundred of it to be laid out in his funeral procession . . ."

In 1698 Bristol was visited by one of the most remarkable of all seventeenth century travellers, the intrepid Celia Fiennes, who in spite of all hardships and dangers, journeyed over most of England, recording and commenting upon all that she saw. She already had a family connection with Bristol, although an unhappy one, for her father, Nathaniel Fiennes, a prominent Parliamentarian and a Colonel in the Parliamentary army during the Civil War, was governor of Bristol in 1643 until forced to surrender the city to the Royalists under Prince Rupert after a fierce attack. The loss of Bristol in 1643 had been a severe blow to the Parliamentary cause and a great encouragement to the Royalists, and Colonel Fiennes was tried by Court Martial and sentenced to death for surrendering the city, although he was eventually pardoned. Celia Fiennes came to Bristol from Bath, travelling through Kingswood, and it is an indication of the bad state of the roads that she noted that coal was brought from Kingswood collieries to Bristol on the backs of large numbers of packhorses, since carts would soon have stuck fast in the muddy, rutted tracks.

In Bristol itself Celia Fiennes found many of the streets very narrow and dark, having tall wooden buildings on either side with overhanging upper storeys which kept out the light. She commented upon the numerous churches and almshouses, especially the fine almshouse which had been founded on St Michael's Hill by the merchant and philanthropist Edward Colston in 1690. By the Market Place she saw 'an Exchange set on stone pillars', and she noted the fine High Cross in the centre of the city, and the open area of the Marsh upon which Queen's Square was soon to be built but which in 1698 was 'encompassed with trees on either side which are lofty and shady', and which was used by 'the Company of the town to take the diversion of walking in the evening'. Above all Celia Fiennes was impressed by the busy port, "This town is a very great tradeing citty as most in England, and is esteemed the largest next London; the river Aven, that is flowed up by the sea into the Severn and soe up the Aven to the town, beares shipps and barges up to the key, where I saw the harbour was full of shipps carrying coales and all sortes of commodityes to other parts; the Bridge is built over with houses just as London Bridge is, but it is not so bigg or long, there are 4 large arches here; they use little boates called Wherryes such as we use on the Thames, soe they use them here to convey persons from place to place; and in many places there are signes to many houses that are not Publick houses just as it is in London; the streetes are well pitch'd and preserved by their using sleds to carry all things about."[9]

Notes

1. Peter Mundy, Travels in Europe and Asia 1608-1667, *Hakluyt Society*, Series II, LV, 1925, 8-11.
2. T B Howell (ed.), *Complete Collection of State Trials*, 1817, IV, 229.
3. W D Macray (ed.), *Clarendon's History of the Rebellion and Civil Wars in England*, 1888, ii, 294-5.
4. Eliot Warburton, *Memoirs of Prince Rupert and the Cavaliers*, 1849, iii, 181.
5. W C Abbott, *The Writings and Speeches of Oliver Cromwell*, 1937, i, 374-9.
6. E S de Beer (ed.), *The Diary of John Evelyn*, 1955, 111, 102-3.
7. Thomas Fuller, *The Worthies of England*, 1952 edition, 504-10.
8. Robert Latham and William Matthews (eds.), *The Diary of Samuel Pepys*, 1976 edition, IX, 224-36.
9. Christopher Morris (ed.), *The Journeys of Celia Fiennes*, 1949, 237-40.

Other Sources

L G Wickham Legg (ed.), A Relation of a Short Survey of Twenty-Six Counties in 1634, *Camden Society*, 1904, 92-8.
J E Pritchard, The Great Plan of Bristol 1673, *Bristol and Gloucestershire Archaeological Society Transactions*, 44, 1922, 203-20.
Joshua Sprigg, *Anglia Rediviva*, 1854, 97-131.
P McGrath, *Bristol and the Civil War*, Bristol Historical Association, 1981.
J Latimer, *Annals of Bristol in the Seventeenth Century*, 1903.
M D Lobel and E M Carus Wilson, *Historic Towns — Bristol*, 1975.

FOUR

EIGHTEENTH CENTURY ACCOUNTS
'Cloudy Looks and Busy Faces'

The eighteenth century was the golden age of Bristol when it was at the height of its prosperity, the leading English port outside London and the 'metropolis of the west', possessed of thriving industries and at the centre of a great commercial network. It was a century of rapid growth in population and in the extent of the city. Population grew from about 20,000 in 1700 to 68,000 in 1801; the city expanded into Queen's Square, across the Frome and westward up the hillside to Brandon Hill and Kingsdown, with fine new streets such as Park Street and Great George Street, while the development of the spa at Hotwells which for a time achieved a national reputation, led to a building boom there and at Clifton. The trade of the port expanded rapidly during the eighteenth century as new markets and new sources of supply were opened up in the New World and especially in the West Indies with which Bristol developed the closest links. The staple commodities of trade through the port were sugar, cocoa, tobacco, wine and glass. Visitors came to participate in the flourishing trade and commerce and in the multitude of Bristol industries, to take ship for foreign ports, to seek health and diversion at the increasingly fashionable Hotwells spa, or to visit the smart and rapidly expanding village of Clifton with its healthy downs and sublime gorge. By the end of the century, however, it was already apparent that trade in the port of Bristol was being outstripped by the rapid development of Liverpool, and that Bristol's position as the second city of the country was being lost to new manufacturing centres such as Birmingham and Manchester.

One of the most informative accounts of Bristol, its industries and its busy port, was written by Daniel Defoe during the 1720s. Defoe was a journalist recalling the impressions and using the notes he had made on journeys throughout England during the previous decade. His interests lay particularly in trade, industry and economic life, in the rich pattern of contemporary society, in religious life and especially in the increasing number of those who, like himself, were non-conformists or dissenters; above all Defoe was fascinated by the new processes, new discoveries and inventions. Naturally therefore Bristol interested him greatly, and in an often-quoted passage he wrote admiringly that it was

"... the greatest, richest and best port of trade in Great Britain, London only excepted. The merchants of this city not only have the greatest trade, but they trade with a more entire independency upon London, than any other town in Britain. And 'tis evident in this particular, (viz.) that whatsoever exportations they make to any part of the world, they are able to bring the full returns back to their own port, and can dispose of it there . . .

. . . the Bristol merchants as they have a very great trade abroad, so they have always buyers at home, for their returns and that such buyers that no cargo is too big for them. To this purpose, the shopkeepers in Bristol who in general are all wholesale men, have so great an inland trade among all the western counties, that they maintain carriers just as the London tradesmen do, to all the principal counties and towns from Southampton in the south, even to the banks of the Trent north; and tho' they have no navigable river that way, yet they drive a very great trade through all those counties."

Defoe also commented upon the importance of the glass-making industry in Bristol,

"There are no less than fifteen glass-houses in Bristol, which is more than are in the city of London: They have indeed a very great expence of glass bottles, by sending them fill'd with beer, cyder, and wine to the West Indies, much more than goes from London; also great numbers of bottles, even such as is almost incredible, are now used for sending the waters of St Vincent's Rock away, which are now carry'd, not all over England only, but, we may say, all over the world."

This busy, flourishing trade of Bristol, and its position as the metropolis for the whole west country and south Wales, as well as the trade up the Severn and the Wye, and the important trading links with Ireland, were what principally impressed Defoe. He admired the energetic Bristol merchants, and the growing town, already so close built that 'there is hardly room to set another house in it', and he was especially pleased by the fine new houses in Queen Square. He was, however, highly critical of the government of

Detail from Buck's South-East Prospect of Bristol, 1734, showing the prominent glass cones in the Temple Street area. Note the fashion of the Negro Page, one of whom, 'Scipio Africanus', is buried in Henbury Churchyard.

Bristol and of the attitude of the Corporation which he believed obstructed the growth of the city and the increase of its trade.

"The greatest inconveniences of Bristol are, its situation, and the tenacious folly of its inhabitants; who by the general infatuation, the pretence of freedoms and priviledges, that corporation-tyranny, which prevents the flourishing and encrease of many a good town in England, continue

63

obstinately to forbid any, who are not subjects of their city soveraignity, (that is to say, freemen,) to trade within the chain of their own liberties; were it not for this, the city of Bristol, would before now, have swell'd and encreas'd in buildings and inhabitants, perhaps to double the magnitude it was formerly of."

Like other visitors, Defoe was impressed by the fine churches, the numerous meeting houses of Dissenters, by the Hot Wells, the water of which he wrote, 'is now famous for being a specifick in the otherwise incurable disease the diabetes . . .', and by Bristol bridge.

"The bridge over the Avon is exceeding strong, the arches very high, because of the depth of water, and the buildings so close upon it, that in passing the bridge, you see nothing but an entire well built street . . . They draw all their heavy goods here on sleds or sledges without wheels, which kills a multitude of horses, and the pavement is worn so smooth by them, that in wet-weather the streets are very slippery, and in frosty-weather 'tis dangerous walking."[1]

The old and picturesque Bristol bridge, which so impressed Defoe and other visitors but which was narrow and inconvenient for carts and wagons, was demolished and replaced by a new bridge in 1761.

The traditional view is that it was while he was in Bristol collecting material for his account of the city that Daniel Defoe met or at least heard the story of Alexander Selkirk who was the original of his famous story *Robinson Crusoe*. Selkirk had been abandoned on the island of Juan Fernandez in the South Seas from where he was rescued by a British captain Woodes Rogers during the course of a privateering voyage.

Another account of early eighteenth-century English towns and cities was produced by Thomas Cox and published piecemeal between 1720 and 1731 under the title *Magna Britannia*. Cox also emphasised the size of Bristol, the extent of its maritime trade and its busy harbour crowded with ships, but gained the impression that Bristolians were totally absorbed in business affairs.

"Bristol is very populous, but the people give themselves up to trade so entirely that nothing of the politeness and gaiety of Bath is to be seen here; all are in a hurry, running up and down with cloudy looks and busy faces, loading, carrying and unloading goods and merchandizes of all sorts from place to place; for the trade of many nations is drawn hither by the industry and opulency of the people.'"[2]

During the eighteenth century the trade of Bristol grew very rapidly indeed, and the prosperity of this 'golden age' in the city's history is still reflected in its buildings and in the spread of its suburbs, especially in the elegant houses built for the wealthy merchants in the heights of Clifton overlooking Bristol and the Avon valley. The growth in trade is also relected in the figures for ships leaving and of merchandise entering the port. During 1687 240 ships left Bristol; by 1717 the figure had risen to 375, and during 1787 it was 448, notwithstanding the fact that the size of ships had increased greatly during the period. The tonnage of goods entering the port also increased substantially from some 20,000 tons during 1700 to about 76,000 tons in 1791. Ships left for many European ports, for North America and the West Indies, Africa and the East Indies. Cargoes brought to Bristol included sugar, rum, dyewoods, wool, cotton, iron, tobacco, wine, fish, fruit and many other commodities. The traffic in slaves dominated the trade of the port for a period during the mid-eighteenth century, and at its peak in 1739 52 Bristol ships were involved, but by the 1770's the number had declined to about 25, and had fallen to only a few ships by the end of the century. Bristol also had very important trading links with Ireland, and a busy traffic in barges with Wales and the ports along the Severn, as well as coastal trade especially with Cornwall, for Cornish copper and calamine from the Mendips formed the raw material of Bristol's important brass industry. Throughout the eighteenth century, it was the busy port and crowded quays, with the many ships in the heart of the city which provided one of the most lasting impressions for visitors to Bristol.

A visitor of an unusual kind ended his short life in Bristol in 1720. We are reminded of the close eighteenth-century connection between Bristol and the horrific traffic in negro slaves by the tomb of a young negro servant who is buried in Henbury churchyard. His name was Scipio Africanus and he was probably not a slave in the generally accepted sense, since the African slaves were taken by Bristol ships directly to the West Indies or to the American plantations for sale; he was rather a page-boy in a wealthy household, for it became fashionable to have such boys with high-sounding Roman names as curiosities, alongside the more usual footmen. The inscription on the tomb of this unfortunate boy does however serve to draw attention to the part played by Bristol ships

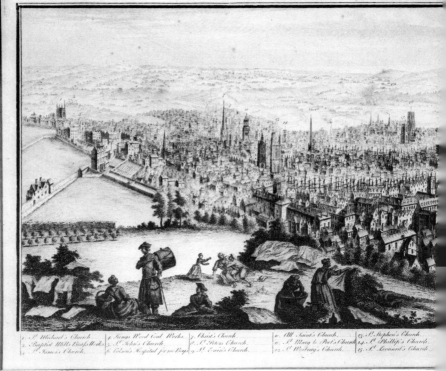

Buck's North-West Prospect of 1734 from Brandon Hill. Th
Brandon Hill was ap

in this evil trade and illuminates the contemporary attitude to
negroes.

Here
Lieth the Body of
S C I P I O   A F R I C A N U S
Negro Servant to ye Right
Honourable Charles William
Earl of Suffolk and Bradon
Who died Ye 21 December
1720 Aged 18 years
I who was Born a PAGAN and a SLAVE
Now sweetly sleep a CHRISTIAN in my Grave,

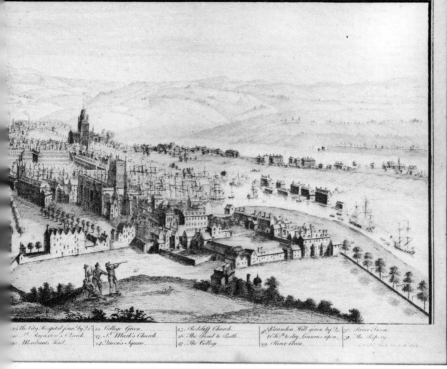

with ships, emphasising the enormous scale of trade in the city.
te spot for drying clothes

What tho' my hue was dark my SAVIOUR'S sight
Shall change this darkness into radiant Light.
Such grace to me my Lord on earth has given
To recommend me to my Lord in heaven,
Whose glorious second coming here I wait
With Saints and Angels Him to celebrate.

In 1739 the poet and satirist Alexander Pope came to Hotwells having been advised by his doctors that his ill-health would 'be mended by drinking the Waters warm at Bristol'. He was greatly struck by the sight of the flourishing Bristol glassworks, with their great cones or pyramids in which the glass was fired and which were such a prominent feature of the Bristol landscape. He wrote to his friend Martha Blount,

67

"I hardly knew what I undertook when I said I would give you some Account of this place. Nothing can do it but a Picture, it is so unlike any Scene you ever saw. But I'll begin at least, and reserve the rest to my next letter. From Bath you go along the River, or its Side, the Road lying generally in sight of it, on each Bank are steep rising Hills cloathed with Wood at top, and sloping toward the stream in Green Meadows, intermixt with white Houses, Mills & Bridges, this for 7 & 8 miles, then you come in sight of Bristol, the River winding at the bottom of steeper banks to the Town where you see twenty odd Pyramids smoking over the Town (which are Glasshouses) and a vast Extent of Houses red & white. You come first to Old Walls, & over a Bridge built on both sides like London bridge, and as much crowded, with a stronge mixture of Seamen, women, children, loaded Horses, Asses, & Sledges with Goods dragging along, all together, without posts to seperate them. From thence you come to a Key along the old Wall with houses on both sides, and in the middle of the street, as far as you can see, hundreds of Ships, their Masts as thick as they can stand by one another, which is the oddest & most surprising sight imaginable. This street is fuller of them, than the Thames from London Bridge to Deptford, & at certain times only, the Water rises to carry them out; so that at other times, a Long Street full of ships in the Middle & Houses on both sides looks like a Dream. Passing still along by the River you come to a Rocky way on one Side, overlooking green Hills on the other; On that rocky way rise several white Houses, and over them red rocks, and as you go further, more Rocks above rocks, mixed with green bushes, and of different coloured stone. This at a Mile's end, terminates in the House of the Hot well, whereabouts lye several pretty Lodging Houses open to the River with Walks of Trees."

Alexander Pope was not greatly impressed either by the efficacy of the water or by the facilities at Hotwells. In November 1739 he wrote,

"I believe the Bristol waters at the Well, would be serviceable if I could stay long enough, viz. six weeks or two months, for as they are an Alternative, and of no great strength, they require a longer time to operate than warmer and more impregnated Mineral-Waters such as Bath etc. The place is so Exposed, and so inconvenient for want of Chairs, Coaches at all easy, etc., that is no living long here in winter for such thin bodies as mine."

Pope was, however, attracted by the village of Clifton with its pretty lodging houses, fine walks and superb view of the Gorge and across to Wales. But the character of the citizens of Bristol did not appeal to him at all,

"The City of Bristol itself is very unpleasant and no civilized Company in it. Only the Collector of the Customs would have brought me acquainted with the Merchants, of whom I hear no great Character. The streets are as crowded as London but the best Image I can give you of it is 'Tis as if Wapping and Southwark were ten-times as big, or all their people run into London. Nothing is fine in it but the Square, which is larger than Grosvenor-Square and wellbuilded, with a very fine brass Statue in the middle of King William on Horseback; And the Key which is full of ships and goes half round this Square. The College Green is pretty and (like the Square) set with trees, with a very fine Old Cross of Gothic curious work in the middle, but spoild with the folly of new gilding it, that takes away all the venerable Antiquity. There is a Cathedral very neat, and 19 parish Churches."[3]

At the end of March 1739, John Wesley arrived in Bristol to visit the great evangelist and preacher George Whitefield, and, inspired by Whitefield's example, Wesley was to begin in Bristol that preaching ministry which was to last for the next fifty years, and was to have such a profound effect upon the whole of England. Bristol remained a principal centre of John Wesley's work, and his brother, Charles Wesley, lived in Bristol from 1749 to 1771 and there wrote many of his best-loved hymns. In his *Journal* John Wesley described his arrival in Bristol and his tentative, doubtful attempts at open-air preaching which took place at 'a little eminence' near a brickyard in St Philip's Marsh, in an area to the east of the city where there remained much open space.

"Saturday 31 March 1739

In the evening I reached Bristol, and met Mr Whitefield there. I could scarce reconcile myself at first to this strange way of preaching in the fields, of which he set me an example on Sunday; having been all my life (till very lately) so tenacious of every point relating to decency and order, that I should have thought the saving of souls almost a sin if it had not been done in a church.

Sunday 1 April 1739

In the evening Mr Whitefield being gone, I begun expounding Our Lord's Sermon on the Mount (one pretty remarkable precedent of field preaching, though I suppose there were churches at that time also) to a little society which was accustomed to meet once or twice a week in Nicholas Street.

Monday 2 April 1739

At four in the afternoon I submitted to be more vile, and proclaimed in the highways the glad tidings of salvation, speaking from a little eminence in a ground adjoining to the city to about three thousand people . . .

At seven I began expounding the Acts of the Apostles to a society meeting in Baldwin Street; and the next day the Gospel of St John in the chapel at Newgate, where I also daily read the Morning Service of the Church.

Sunday 8 April 1739

At seven in the morning I preached to about a thousand persons at Bristol, and afterwards to about fifteen hundred on the top of Hanham Mount in Kingswood . . ."

John Wesley soon found that because of the success of his preaching in Bristol he was much more heavily involved and financially committed than ever he had intended when he first visited the city a few weeks earlier.

"Wednesday 9 May 1739

We took possession of a piece of ground, near St James's churchyard, in the Horsefair, where it was designed to build a room, large enough to contain both the societies of Nicholas and Baldwin Street, and such of their acquaintance as might desire to be present with them, at such times as the Scripture was expounded. And on Saturday the 12th the first stone was laid, with the voice of praise and thanksgiving.

I had not at first the least apprehension or design of being personally engaged, either in the expenses of this work or in the direction of it; having appointed eleven feoffees, on whom I supposed these burdens would fall of course. But I quickly found my mistake; first with regard to the expense: for the whole undertaking must have stood still had I not immediately taken upon myself the payment of all the workmen; so that, before I knew where I was, I had contracted a debt of more than a hundred and fifty pounds. And this I was to discharge how I could; the subscriptions of both societies not amounting to one quarter of the sum. And as to the direction of the work, I presently received letters from my friends in London, Mr Whitefield in particular, backed by a message from one just come from thence, that neither he nor they would have anything to do with the building neither contribute anything towards it, unless I would instantly discharge all feoffees and do everything in my own name. Many reasons they gave for this; but one was enough, viz. "that such feoffees always would have it in their power to control me, and if I had preached not as they liked, to turn me out of the room I had built." I accordingly yielded to their advice, and, calling all the feoffees together, cancelled (no man opposing) the instrument made before, and took the whole management into my own hands. Money it is true, I had not, nor any human prospect or probability of procuring it; but I knew 'the earth is the Lord's

John Wesley's New Room in Broadmead, begun in 1739: an event which marked the real beginnings of Methodism.

71

and the fulness thereof', and in His name set out, nothing doubting."[4]

This momentous decision of John Wesley's resulted in the building of the New Room which still survives in Broadmead, and in many ways marks the real beginnings of Methodism, with all its tremendous implications, both religious and social. For the rest of his long life John Wesley was to make regular visits to Bristol, and nowhere in England was more important in the early growth and development of the Methodist movement. But in spite of his successful preaching in Bristol, and the fact that his brother, Charles Wesley, had for many years lived in the city, John Wesley remained disappointed by Bristolians, and in a letter of 1790 wrote to his friend:

"I often wonder at the people of Bristol. They are so honest, yet so dull; 'tis scarce possible to strike any fire into them."[5]

The growing reputation and popularity of Hotwells as a spa and as a resort meant that entertainments as well as lodging houses had to be established at Jacob's Wells, then outside the city and conveniently placed for Hotwells and Clifton, by the famous comedian, John Hippisley, in 1729, and some of the greatest actors and actresses of the period appeared there. The continued expansion of the spa and the growing prosperity of Bristol led to the foundation of the theatre in King Street, which was to become the Theatre Royal; building began in 1764 and the theatre opened in 1766. Theatres were still regarded by many religious and pious persons as evil influences, and John Wesley strongly endorsed this belief. Accordingly in 1764 he wrote to the Mayor and Corporation unsuccessfully urging them to ban the proposed theatre,

"To the Mayor and Corporation of Bristol

London, December 20, 1764

Gentlemen, Both my brother and I and all who have any connexion with us are extremely sensible of our obligations to you for the civility which you have shown us on all occasions; and we cannot but feel ourselves deeply interested in whatever we apprehend in any degrees to concern your honour or the general good and prosperity of the City of Bristol. This occasions my giving you the present trouble, which (whether it has any farther effect or no) you will please to receive as a testimony of the high regard we shall ever retain for you.

The endeavours lately used to procure subscriptions for

building a new playhouse in Bristol have given us not a little concern; and that on various accounts: not barely as most of the present stage entertainments sap the foundation of all religion, as they naturally tend to efface all traces of piety and seriousness out of the minds of men; but as they are peculiarly hurtful to a trading city, giving a wrong turn to youth especially gay, trifling, and directly opposite to the spirit of industry and close application to business; and, as drinking and debauchery of every kind are constant attendants on these entertainments, with indolence, effeminacy, and idleness, which affect trade in a high degree.''

In spite of the opposition from Wesley and others, and from Quakers, including Richard Champion, a member of an important Bristol family of merchants and traders, nonetheless the King Street theatre was a great success, and eventually obtained a royal licence in 1778 and became the Theatre Royal.

As the population of Bristol grew during the eighteenth century, the central area of the city, especially within the circuit of the medieval walls, grew ever more crowded, for in spite of the rapid suburban growth and the tremendous development of Clifton, nonetheless houses, shops, factories and workshops were crammed ever more tightly together within the old core of the city. A consequence was that Bristol became an increasingly unhealthy place in which to live and work, and cholera, typhoid and other diseases were rife. Another possible consequence of the crowded conditions was suggested by a government agent, R J Sullivan, who visited the city frequently during the 1770s.

"When we consider Bristol as a place of trade and riches we are greatly surprised to find the houses so meanly built, and the streets so narrow, dirty, and ill-paved. This is in some measure owing to an ill-judged parsimony; for the houses being mostly built in the same manner as those in London before the Fire of 1666, with the upper storeys projecting in the streets, are patched up and repaired from time to time—But this is a very impolitic measure; for besides the expenses attending the different repairs, and the low price of the rents, were a fire to happen in Bristol, it would be attended with as dreadful consequences, in proportion to the number of inhabitants, as it was in London."[6]

To escape from residence in the central area into the expanding suburbs became the ambition of those who could afford to do so, and the eighteenth century witnessed an end to the old practice whereby all classes of society lived closely packed into the same area, and saw the richer classes depart into new, elegant houses away from the noise, bustle and stench of the city and the harbour. This is made clear in a description of Bristol published in the *Gentleman's Magazine* in 1789.

> "The best-built parts of Bristol are College-green, some of the streets in the neighbourhood of the green, and Queen Square. The suburb called King's-down abounds with good houses; and as this part stands pleasantly in an elevated situation, removed in some degree from the smoke and noise of the city, additions are frequently made to the number of its inhabitants."

One of the Bristol merchant dynasties who established an elegant house and garden outside the city was the Quaker family of Goldney whose house was at Clifton on the hill overlooking Bristol and the Avon valley with views south and west into Somerset. The Goldney family had been Bristol merchants since the later seventeenth century, and had extensive business interests in shipping, banking and manufacturing, including an important share in Abraham Darby's iron works at Coalbrookdale in Shropshire. From the late seventeenth century, three successive members of this family of devout and dedicated Quaker businessmen, each of whom was called Thomas Goldney, established the family fortunes to such an extent that a house and land on the hill-top at Clifton was leased in 1694 and purchased outright in 1705.

During the 1720s the house was rebuilt, and from about 1730 onwards Thomas Goldney III acquired more land and laid out the garden which soon became well-known for its trees and plants which included many rare species as well as oranges, lemons, vines, flowering shrubs, trees and flowers. Although covering a relatively small area, the garden was also provided with water-works, a fountain worked by a steam engine, terraces, a tower, gazebo, rotunda and, most famous and spectacular of all, with a superb grotto decorated with statues, carvings and with innumerable sea-shells and pieces of coral. The grotto bears the date 1739, although it is likely that

Opposite: The classic 18th century garden at Goldney House. The purpose of the tower was to provide a decorative water pump for the fountain and grotto.

further work was done on it after that date, and Thomas Goldney continued to add to and embellish his garden up to the time of his death in 1768.

Not surprisingly the remarkable garden soon became well-known and entry was much sought after by the gentry and tourists who came to Hotwells and Clifton. Thomas Goldney therefore began the practice of issuing tickets which enabled visitors to be conducted around the garden and grotto by his gardener, Adam Sixsmith.

This custom continued after Thomas Goldney's death and in 1778 one of those who obtained a ticket to see the garden was the American loyalist, Samuel Curwen, who had sought refuge in England after the Declaration of Independence. In his *Journal* he described his visit to the garden as follows:

"Knocking at the gate we were soon admitted and attended by the gardner was conducted through the garden walks, which are kept in the nicest order; the whole having an appearance of care, attention and industry. 'Tis on a moderate scale but well filled with orange, lemon trees, etc. and a small piece of water abounding in gold and silver fish, supplyed from a natural fountain by a lofty fire Engine erected at one end of the terrass walk; the stream runs underground for a small distance, and discharges itself through an urn, on which a Neptune rests with his trident—the ground between it and the engine made rough, scraggy and woody to resemble a wilderness. Going through the main walk, we arrived at the Door of the Grotto, situated under the terrass; the first object that presented itself to our view was a lion sitting; and behind, in a dark cave a lioness; the latter so much resembling life that I could hardly persuade myself to the contrary. The form of the Grotto is octangular or circular, its roof a semi-circle, a dome, in the center atop is a round window, the diameter about 18 or 20 feet from the door in front to the mouth of the Cave in which the Lioness sits. On each side to the right and left of the entrance the roof is supported by gyral pillars, covered, as its sides and roof are, with an incredible variety of shells, stones, sparrs, petrifactions, etc., etc., the mountains, nay, even, the bowels of the earth, to the shores of the sea, the bottom also of it seems to have been pillaged to furnish materials to adorn this curious subterranean recess."[7]

In 1747 another Bristol merchant and shipowner, Paul Fisher, built an elegant house near Goldney at Clifton Hill House on the Clifton hillside overlooking Bristol. It was designed by a London architect, Isaac Ware, and remains one of the finest examples of a Palladian building in Bristol, and its elegant rooms and fine garden illustrate the wealth of Bristol merchants and the way in which so many of them moved out of the crowded conditions of the city to the clearer air and rural surroundings of Clifton.

In the autumn of 1766 the author and amateur architect, Horace Walpole, who had transformed his house at Twickenham into the well-known and much-visited mock-Gothic castle of Strawberry Hill, came to Bristol, and commented upon the similar mock-Gothic buildings at Arnos Court. These had been built during 1760-65 by the Quaker copper-merchant, William Reeves, who used the blocks of black slag from his smelting works together with lighter coloured stone dressings to construct 'Arnos Castle' which housed the stables and outbuildings. Walpole had been to Bath to take the waters, and complained bitterly that he had not enjoyed his visit, neither the place nor the company.

"22 October 1766

They may say what they will, but it does one ten times more good to leave Bath than to go to it . . .

I did go to Bristol, the dirtiest great shop I ever saw, with so foul a river, that had I seen the least appearance of cleanliness, I should have concluded they washed all their linen in it, as they do at Paris. Going into the town, I was struck with a large Gothic building, coal black, and striped with white; I took it for the devil's cathedral. When I came nearer I found it was a uniform castle, lately built, and serving for stables and offices to a smart false-Gothic house on the other side of the road. The real cathedral is very neat and has pretty tombs . . ."[8]

Among the literary figures who visited the Hotwells spa at the height of its popularity during the eighteenth century, were Addison, Cowper, Gay and Sheridan as well as the poet, Alexander Pope, whose comments on the spa and on Clifton have already been quoted.

On 29 April 1776 Dr Samuel Johnson and his biographer, James Boswell, visited Bristol. Their visit was at a time of continuing public controversy over the authenticity of the mock-medieval poems and 'ancient' documents produced by the tragic Bristol poet Thomas Chatterton. Chatterton had left Bristol for London in 1770, and after four months in the capital had dashed his hopes of instant literary fame, he had taken his own life. Several Bristolians were convinced by Chatterton's fraudulent claims, among them the pewter-maker and antiquarian, George Catcot, and the surgeon William Barrett who later wrote a history of Bristol, published in 1789. Dr Johnson was in no doubt that the poems and writings which Chatterton claimed were the work of William Canynges and another fifteenth-century Bristolian, Thomas Rowley, were in fact the work of Chatterton himself, and declared his opinion with his customary vigour. Boswell's account is as follows:

"On Monday 29 April (1776) he and I made an excursion to Bristol, where I was entertained with seeing him enquire upon the spot, into the authenticity of 'Rowley's Poetry', as I had seen him enquire upon the spot into the authenticity of 'Ossian's Poetry'. George Catcot, the pewterer, who was as zealous for Rowley, as Dr Hugh Blair was for Ossian, (I trust my Reverend friend will excuse the comparison) attended us at our inn, and with a triumphant air of lively simplicity called out, 'I'll make Dr Johnson a convert.' Dr Johnson, at his desire read aloud some of Chatterton's fabricated verses, while Catcot stood at the back of his chair, moving himself like a pendulum, and beating time with his feet, and now and then looking into Dr Johnson's face, wondering that he was not yet convinced. We called on Mr Barret, the surgeon, and saw some of the *originals* as they were called, which were executed very artificially; but from a careful inspection of them, and a consideration of the circumstances with which they were attended, we were quite satisfied of the imposture, which, indeed, has been clearly demonstrated from internal evidence, by several able criticks.

Honest Catcot seemed to pay no attention whatever to any objections, but insisted, as an end of all controversy, that we should go with him to the tower of the church of St Mary, Redcliff, and view with our own eyes the ancient chest in which the manuscripts were found. To this, Dr Johnson good-naturedly agreed; and though troubled with a shortness of breathing, laboured up a long flight of steps, till we came to the place where the wonderous chest stood. 'There, (said Catcot, with a bouncing confident credulity) there is the very chest itself.' After this ocular demonstration, there was no more to be said. He brought to my recollection a Scotch Highlander, a man of learning too, and who had seen the world, attesting, and at the same time giving his reasons for the authenticity of Fingal:- 'I have heard all that poem when I was young.'— 'Have you, Sir? Pray what have you heard?'—'I have heard Ossian, Oscar, and every one of them.'

Johnson said of Chatterton, 'This is the most extraordinary young man that has encountered my knowledge. It is wonderful how the whelp has written such things.'

We were by no means pleased with our inn at Bristol. 'Let us see now (said I) how we should describe it.' Johnson was ready with his raillery. 'Describe it, Sir?—Why, it was so bad that Boswell wished to be in Scotland!'"[9]

During the eighteenth century the spa at Hotwells became well-known as a health resort and for a time began to rival Bath as a medicinal and social centre. As early as 1626 Sir Hugh Smyth of Ashton Court was rising early to go to the wells and drink the medicinal waters, and in 1667 Queen Catherine, wife of Charles II, drank the waters there during her visit to Bristol. In 1712 Sir Robert Atkyns, the historian of Gloucestershire, whose father had been Recorder of Bristol, wrote that the Hot Well was 'famous for curing divers distempers, especially the diabetes.'

In 1723, Sarah, Duchess of Marlborough, was one of a growing stream of notable visitors, while bottled supplies of the water were already being shipped from Bristol to London, creating another lucrative market for Bristol glass bottles. As more visitors and invalids arrived to take the waters and to benefit from the bracing air and picturesque walks of Clifton, lodging-houses, and amusements had to be provided for their entertainment. In 1758 Dr Sutherland of Bath, gave a long description of *The Nature and Qualities of Bristol Water,* and remarked on the attractions of the district,

". . . provisions of all sorts are to be had in plenty, during the Summer, which is the season allotted by custom for drinking these Waters. Garden Stuff is early and excellent. There are Lodgings near the Wells, convenient for such as are real Invalids; there are magnificent Lodgings in the beautiful village of Clifton, on the top of the hill, for such as have carriages, and whose lungs can bear a keener air. There are Balls twice a week, and Card-playing every night."

Genteel Hotwells and Clifton before the bridge, c1830.

During the later eighteenth century the popularity of the spa reached its height. The Duke of York took the waters in 1766 and was followed by many of the nobility and gentry, so that it became one of the most popular and crowded of all the many English spas. The number of Clifton lodging houses, inns and places of entertainment grew accordingly, and music, dancing, card-playing, walks on the Downs and trips on the river were provided for the guests. A Bristol guide of 1793 also noted another popular diversion

> ". . . many ladies and gentlemen cross the River at Rownham Ferry and walk to the sweet and wholesome village of Ashton to eat strawberries and raspberries with cream; a delicious repast."

The massive expansion of Clifton did not please everyone, and Lady Hesketh wrote in 1799 that

> "the Bristol people have done all in their power to ruin the rural beauties of Clifton Hill by the number of abominable Buildings they have erected all over it."

But even so, she was charmed by the fine views over woods, water and rocks, and thought that

> "it is always preferable to any other place."

The prosperity of Bristol during the eighteenth century, and the growth of the city and its suburbs, is reflected in the growing number of published maps and plans, and in the Directories which list the prominent residents, merchants, ship-owners and industrialists. James Millerd's map of Bristol of 1673 has already been referred to, and there were several subsequent editions; in 1742 Jean Roque's *Plan of Bristol* was published at the very large scale of 26 inches to 1 mile. Roque was a Frenchman, living in England, and his huge map is particularly useful for identifying streets, houses, inns and other buildings, many of which have long since disappeared. In 1773 Benjamin Donn or Donne produced a *Plan* at a scale of 8 inches to 1 mile. In 1765 Donne was appointed librarian of the old city library in King Street, an appointment which apparently left him with plenty of leisure, since he was able to establish a school for mathematics on the premises, and to undertake the surveys for his map. When it was published the city council rewarded him with a gift of twenty guineas. Donne also left a brief description of the inconvenience of Bristol as a port and of the difficulties caused both to shipping and to the inhabitants by the tidal flow.

"Two Navigable Rivers flow thro' Bristol—the Avon and the Froom. The Avon is the principal, and is capable of floating a seventy four Gun Ship at the Quay. This River, to which Bristol is indebted for its Origin, and support, has at low Water, a very unpleasing appearance, Being filled with a disagreeable Slimy Mud—A Stranger upon viewing the Avon at Ebb Tide is generally struck with astonishment and can scarcely conceive it possible for Ships of any Burden to approach the City, by so insignificant a Gut (it being at no part a Furlong in Width—and in the Summer it is almost dry at low Water). But the improbability ceases when he is informed that at Spring tide the Water rises at Pill 40 feet—and sometimes overflows Bristol key and even runs into the Neighbouring Houses . . ."

In 1794 W Matthews published a map of Bristol and its suburbs including for the first time Clifton and Hotwells, showing the dramatic growth in houses as a result of the development of the Spa and of the lodging houses and private dwellings in Clifton. Matthews also published one of the early Bristol Directories; others included Sketchley's 1775, Shiercliff's 1785, Routh's 1787, Reed's 1791. Matthews' Directory was the longest-lived and provides a continuous picture of the changes in Bristol during the late eighteenth and early nineteenth centuries.

Among those who came to live in Clifton during the late eighteenth century was Dr Thomas Beddoes who came there from Oxford in 1793, with a high reputation for his studies in medicine and chemistry. In Clifton he continued his experimental work on the use of various gases, including nitrous oxide or 'laughing gas', in the treatment of diseases such as consumption. Since Clifton and Hotwells were much frequented by consumptives they were an ideal situation for his work.

In October 1798 the Cornishman, Humphry Davy, who was later to achieve great fame as the inventor of the miners' safety lamp, came from Penzance to assist Beddoes in the running of the 'Pneumatic Institution' which was first established in Hope Square, and later moved to Dowry Square. Writing to his mother a few days after his arrival, Humphry Davy enthusiastically described his new home in Clifton,

"Clifton is situated on the top of a hill, commanding a view of Bristol and its neighbourhood, conveniently elevated above the dirt and noise of the city. Here are houses, rocks, woods, town and country in one small spot; and beneath us the sweetly-flowing Avon, so celebrated by the poets. Indeed, there can hardly be a more beautiful spot; it almost rivals Penzance and the beauties of Mount's Bay.

Our house is capacious and handsome; my rooms are very large, nice, and convenient; and, above all, I have an excellent laboratory."

Another person associated with Dr Beddoes in Clifton was his father-in-law, Richard Lovell Edgeworth; one of Edgeworth's daughters was the popular novelist, Maria Edgeworth, who was a frequent visitor to Clifton. In 1793 she stayed with her father at Prince's Buildings, and in a letter to her uncle she wrote,

"We live very near the Downs, where we have almost every day charming walks, and all the children go bounding about over hill and dale along with us . . .

My father has got a transfer of a ticket for the Bristol Library, which is an extremely fine one, and what makes it appear ten times finer is that it is very difficult for strangers to get into. From thence he can get almost any book for us when he pleases, except a few of the most scarce, which are, by the laws of the library, immovable. No ladies go to the library; but Mr

Johnes, the librarian, is very civil, and my mother went to his rooms and saw the beautiful prints in Boydell's *Shakespeare.*"

The Bristol Library was the oldest provincial library in England, and had been started in 1613 by a Bristol merchant, Robert Redwood. It was situated in a fine building in King Street. In another letter to her uncle, Maria Edgeworth refers to Ann Yearsley, the poor woman who had kept cows and sold milk on Clifton Down, and whose poetry achieved a rapid but transitory popularity after she was befriended and helped by the author and philanthropist, Hannah More.

"Mrs Yearsley, the milkwoman, whose poems I daresay my aunt has seen, lives near us at Clifton. We have never seen her, and probably never shall; for my father is so indignant against her for her ingratitude to her benefactress, Miss Hannah More, that he thinks she deserves to be treated with neglect."

Like many others, including the poets Coleridge and Southey, Maria Edgeworth tried the effects of inhaling nitrous oxide or 'laughing gas' at her brother-in-law's 'Pneumatic Institution', and she was enthusiastic about its results.

"A young man, a Mr Davy, at Dr Beddoes's, who has applied himself much to chemistry, has made some discoveries of importance, and enthusiastically expects wonders will be performed by the use of certain gases, which inebriate in the most delightful manner, having the oblivious effects of Lethe, and at the same time giving the rapturous sensations of the Nectar of the Gods!"

Robert Southey also tried the effects of the gas and wrote to his brother in 1799 that 'Davy has actually invented a new pleasure, for which language has no name.'[10]

There are many descriptions of Bristol and its environs written by wealthy and cultured visitors to Clifton and Hotwells, and the society of the spa figures in several eighteenth century novels, notably in Smollett's *Humphry Clinker* and Fanny Burney's *Evelina.* But it is much more difficult to find descriptions of *working* Bristol, or of the seamen, labourers and the poor who made up by far the largest section of Bristol population. It is as a reminder of this other important aspect of Bristol society that these final examples in this chapter have been chosen.

The most hideous, insanitary and appalling place in eighteenth-century Bristol was undoubtedly the Bristol gaol, known as Newgate. This had remained since the Middle Ages by the walls of Bristol castle, on the low-lying ground between the castle moat and the river Frome, in cramped, damp and unhealthy surroundings. John Wesley in 1761 compared the Bristol prison unfavourably with the notorious London prison of the same name,

"Of all the seats of woe on this side of hell, few, I suppose, exceed or even equal (London) Newgate. If any region of horror could exceed it a few years ago, Newgate in Bristol did; so great was the filth, the stench, the misery, and wickedness which shocked all who had a spark of humanity left."

In 1777 the prison reformer, John Howard, visited Bristol to collect material for his great enquiry into the state of English prisons. Howard made several visits to the Newgate gaol, and found that the small, ill-ventilated rooms and tiny passages contained thirty-eight felons and fifty-eight debtors. The atmosphere was offensive, and was made worse by the open sewers. There was insufficient water and inadequate food for the prisoners.

Howard also noted that there was no proper separation between men and women prisoners, nor between debtors and felons, so that 'the debtors mix in diversions with the felons, by which they become more daring and wicked than the felons.'

In the centre of the prison was a dungeon, a pit seventeen feet in diameter and eight and a half feet high, where no bedding or straw was provided, and there was only one small window. Not surprisingly, Howard found it 'close and offensive'. Nevertheless, in spite of these criticisms, his general conclusion was that the gaol was clean in spite of being so crowded and close, but that 'the utmost attention is required to keep the prison healthy'.

Of John Howard's noble and self-sacrificing work to improve the generally appalling conditions in English prisons, the great Bristol member of Parliament, Edmund Burke, wrote memorably that Howard had undertaken.

". . . to dive into the depths of dungeons; to plunge into the infection of hospitals, to survey the mansions of sorrow and pain; to take the gauge and dimensions of misery, depression, and contempt; to remember the forgotten, to attend to the neglected, to visit the forsaken, and to compare and collate the distresses of all men in all countries."

In 1787 a young clergyman, Thomas Clarkson, came to Bristol in order to collect evidence concerning the slave trade in which Bristol ships and seamen played an important part. This was the beginning of Clarkson's work on behalf of the Committee for the Abolition of the Slave Trade, work which eventually, after a long and bitter struggle lasting for twenty years, was to be successful when Parliament declared the trade illegal in 1806. At the start of this long and arduous campaign, when final success seemed remote and unlikely, Clarkson recorded his feelings as he came within sight of Bristol.

"The first place I resolved to visit was Bristol . . . On turning a corner within about a mile of that city, at about eight in the evening, I came within sight of it. The weather was rather hazy, which occasioned it to look of unusual dimensions. The bells of some of the churches were then ringing; the sound of them did not strike me, till I had turned the corner before mentioned, when it came upon me at once. It filled me, almost directly, with a melancholy for which I could not account. I began now to tremble, for the first time, at the arduous task I had undertaken, of attempting to subvert one of the branches of the commerce of the great place which was now before me."

The task upon which Clarkson had embarked was indeed very difficult, and he got little help in Bristol apart from the support of various Quaker families and from a few of the clergy, notably Josiah Tucker, the Dean of Gloucester. At first merchants and sailors were willing to talk to Clarkson about the slave trade, and to condemn its horrors and barbarities, although the profitability of the trade meant that few were willing to support the idea of making it illegal. When his mission became better known, however, he found it increasingly difficult to obtain information. He wrote that

"In my first movements about this city, I found that people talked very openly on the subject of the Slave-trade. They seemed to be well acquainted with the various circumstances belonging to it. There were facts, in short, in every body's mouth, concerning it; and every body seemed to execrate it, though no one thought of its abolition."

Later he was to write,

"The owners of vessels employed in the trade there, forbad all intercourse with me. The old captains, who had made their fortunes in it, would not see me. The young, who were making them, could not be supposed to espouse my cause to the detriment of their own interest."

In spite of all difficulties and threats, however, and although he

Thomas Clarkson, the anti-slavery campaigner.

frequently despaired of success and suffered badly from intense periods of loneliness and depression, Clarkson persisted in collecting evidence. He made repeated visits to the taverns and inns where the sailors lodged and drank when ashore, such as the noisome dens in Marsh Street and St Thomas's Street and elsewhere in the dockside area of the city. For a young and inexperienced clergyman, these visits, the rough company, and the scenes of depravity, vice and debauchery he was compelled to witness were in themselves a fearsome ordeal. He wrote, for example, of one group of lodging houses

> "These houses were in Marsh-street, and most of them were then kept by Irishmen. The scenes witnessed in these houses were truly distressing to me; and yet, if I wished to know practically what I had purposed, I could not avoid them. Music, dancing, rioting, drunkenness and profane swearing were kept up from night to night . . ."[11]

He did receive assistance, however, from the helpful landlord of the 'Seven Stars' tavern, in St Thomas's Street, and slowly he learnt more and more of the slave trade and its barbarities. He learned how the seamen themselves were often very badly treated on the slave ships, and of how they were recruited when drunk or in debt in the Bristol taverns. He also met seamen who were persuaded to take him on board some of the slave ships; and was horrified by their small size and the number of slaves which they were intended to carry. For example a small vessel of only twenty-five tons was destined to carry seventy negro slaves from Africa to the West Indies; while a little sloop of eleven tons which had been built as a pleasure boat to accommodate six persons, was destined to carry thirty slaves. The thirty slaves were to be kept below decks in a space twenty-two feet long and between four and eight feet wide and a mere two feet eight inches high.

After his first visit to Bristol in 1787, Clarkson went on to Liverpool, London and elsewhere to collect evidence; later he was to return to Bristol on several occasions. Meanwhile Bristol's involvement with the slave trade was rapidly declining, and the outbreak of the Napoleonic War, economic difficulties with the West Indies trade and increasing competition from Liverpool, as well as a growing feeling in Bristol that the trade was morally indefensible, all meant that by the time that the slave trade was made illegal in 1806 Bristol ships were no longer heavily involved in it.

Details of the conditions of life for the very poorest classes of society in Bristol are provided by the comprehensive enquiries which were made at the end of the eighteenth century by Sir Frederick Morton Eden and published in 1797 under the title of *The State of the Poor*. During the course of his investigation which took him all over the country, Eden spent some time in Bristol and included in his work a report on the treatment of the poor in the city. He was impressed by the large number of almshouses and charities for the poor which existed in Bristol,

> "Few cities possess such a number of public charities as Bristol. There are 30 alms-houses, in which 83 men and 230 women reside, with an allowance nearly sufficient for their support. There are several charity schools in which about 960 children are educated, and most of them clothed and maintained. The donations to the Poor are considerable, but the exact amount could not be ascertained."[12]

For the very many poor people who were not fortunate enough to secure accommodation in an almshouse, Bristol had as early as 1695 established a workhouse in which they could be housed. This was situated in St Peter's Hospital on the bank of the Avon near St Peter's church, and according to Eden's report the standard of food and accommodation were very basic and left much to be desired. He found that the place housed no fewer than 350 inmates, and that the number a short time before had been as high as 390; some suffered from infectious diseases, and 63 were kept separate in a pest-house; most of the remainder were either old people or children, many were insane, blind or disabled. The only work available for the inmates was picking oakum, that is separating out the fibres of old rope to make material for caulking ships.

> "There are 12 or 15 beds, principally of flocks, in each apartment, for which reason probably, and on account of the number of old and diseased persons in it, the house is infested with vermin, particularly bugs. To a visitor there appears on the whole to be a want of cleanliness."

Eden was an experienced observer who had seen many similar institutions, so that his comments can be accepted as objective and reliable. He also gave details of the meals provided in the Bristol

Opposite: The richly carved facade of St Peter's Hospital, Bristol's most tragic architectural loss in the destruction of the Blitz.

workhouse; clearly the food was very basic and there was little attempt to provide either a varied or a balanced diet.

Bill of Fare

	Breakfast	Dinner	Supper
Sunday	Water-gruel	Soup made of bullock's head	Bread and Cheese
Monday	Water-gruel	Pease-soup	Bread and Cheese
Tuesday	Water-gruel	Meat and Potatoes	Bread and Cheese
Wednesday	Broth	Bread and Cheese	Bread and Cheese
Thursday	Water-gruel	Meat and Potatoes	Bread and Cheese
Friday	Broth	Pease-soup	Bread and Cheese
Saturday	Gruel	Bread and Cheese	Bread and Cheese

In addition to those people accommodated in the Workhouse and in the Almshouses, there were also 1,010 paupers in Bristol who received poor relief in their own homes. Many poor families found it very difficult to exist on their wages at this time (1797) when prices were extraordinarily high because of the Napoleonic War, and were compelled to rely on poor relief to supplement their income. Eden gives as an example the earnings and expenditure of a typical labourer and his wife in Bristol. The man was about 50 years of age and worked as a horse-keeper, porter, etc. at an inn. The details given by Eden are as follows:

"9s 0d a week wages   annually £23 8s 0d
Wife sometimes earns by washing   suppose £1 0s 0d
                                    Total £24 8s 0d
Last summer he lost 2 children by the smallpox; and the summer before he was sick for several months . . . has been obliged to pawn his best cloaths, and some articles of furniture.

Expenses

Bread per week	4s 6d
Meat	6d
Butter ½ lb	5½d
Cheese ½ lb	3d
Tea (no sugar)	3d
Potatoes 2 pecks	1s 0d
Milk ½d per day (for the child)	3½d
Beer (about 3 pints)	6d
Candles, soap, etc.	5d
Onions, salt, etc.	3d
House rent	1s 2d
Fuel	1s 0d
Weekly	10s 9d
Annually	£27 19s 0d

This person appeared to be an honest, industrious man, whose intention was not to deceive."

Finally Eden's brief description of Bristol and its trades sums up many of the changes which had taken place during the eighteenth century.

"Bristol

The extent of the city of Bristol and its liberties is about 3 miles from east to west; and 2½ miles from north to south . . . The great increase in population which has taken place within this present century has been chiefly confined to the out-parishes. Almost half of what is properly called the City has been destroyed to make room for the Exchange, the Market, the Bridge, Clare Street, Union Street, etc.; and although many houses have been built many more have been pulled down . . . many of them have been turned into mere offices for brokers, insurers, attornies, etc., or warehouses for tradesmen, who have in great measure deserted their houses in the town and retired with their families to the neighbouring villages . . . Bristol is not more a commercial than a manufacturing town: independent of the various trades immediately connected with shipping concerns, there are several important manufactures carried on here. Glass-making is the principal. There are near 20 glass-houses in or near the city, for making bottle, crown or flint glass; several works for lead . . ., brass-wire and brass-works; several iron and copper foundries; potteries; two large floor-cloth manufactories; etc. . . . Coals cost about 3½d the bushel: they are chiefly brought from the extensive mines at Kingswood . . . the colliers of which speak a jargon that is peculiar to them, and perfectly unintelligible to a stranger . . . The number of ale-houses in the city of Bristol is 354 . . .''[12]

Notes

1. Daniel Defoe, *Tour Through England and Wales*, Everyman Edition, II.
2. Thomas Cox, *Magna Britannia*, 1720-31.
3. George Sherburn (Ed.) *Correspondence of Alexander Pope*, 1956, IV, 201-5.
4. N Curnock (Ed.), *The Journal of John Wesley*, II, 167-73, III, 32.
5. J Telford (Ed.), *The Letters of John Wesley*, IV, 1931, 279.
6. R J Sullivan, *Observations made during a Tour*, 1780, 91-2; *Gentleman's Magazine*, LIX, 1789, 999.
7. Andrew Oliver (Ed.), *The Journal of Samuel Curwen*, 1972, I, 226.
8. W S Lewis (Ed.), *Horace Walpole's Correspondence*, X, 1941, 232.
9. G B Hill (Ed.), *Boswell's Life of Johnson*, 1887, III, 50-1.
10. *Life and Correspondence of Robert Southey*, 1850, pp 11, 21.
11. T Clarkson, *The History of the Rise, Progress and Accomplishment of the Abolition of the African Slave Trade*, 1808, I, 293-367.
12. A G L Rogers (Ed.), *The State of the Poor by F M Eden*, 1928, 189-92.

Other Sources

Anonymous, *A Complete History of Somerset*, 1742.
John Howard, *The State of the Prisons*, 1777, Everyman Edition, 1927, 227-8.
Percy T Marcy, *Eighteenth Century Views of Bristol and Bristolians*, Bristol Historical Association, 1960.
B Little, *The City and County of Bristol*, 1954.
C M MacInnes, *Bristol and the Slave Trade*, Bristol Historical Association.
P K Stembridge, *Goldney: A House and a Family*, 1969.
Stanley Hutton, *Bristol and Its Famous Associations*, 1907.
J Latimer, *Annals of Bristol during the Eighteenth Century*, 1893.

FIVE

NINETEENTH CENTURY DESCRIPTIONS
'The Third Most Unhealthy Town in England'

Early nineteenth century visitors continued to enthuse over the bustling port of Bristol, the excellence of its situation and buildings and the splendour of the surrounding countryside. In 1803 the poet Robert Southey included a long description of Bristol in *Letters from England* which were published in 1807. Southey had been born in Bristol in 1774, the son of a linendraper in the city. He knew Bristol well, and it was the Bristol bookseller and publisher, Joseph Cottle, who encouraged and supported his early literary efforts as well as those of Coleridge and Wordsworth. The *Letters from England* were published anonymously, and were said to have been written by a Spanish visitor to England and translated into English, but the real author was Southey, who hoped that an account of England apparently written by a foreigner would sell better and make him more profit than a book appearing under his own name. Southey described the approach to Bristol from Bath and Keynsham and the view of the great city set deep in the valley of the Avon—

> "with many steeples, one of which inclines so much from the perpendicular, that I should be sorry to live within reach of its fall,—and the black towers of many glass-houses rolling up black smoke."

In his guise of a Spanish visitor, Southey went on to describe the fine Exchange building in Corn Street, which had been built to the design of John Wood of Bath in 1740-3, and outside it the short brass pillars or 'nails' on which merchants and townsfolk 'might count out their money in their public dealings.' On one of the 'nails' Southey observed a man selling newspapers and on another a cage of goldfinches was exposed for sale. He commented also on the busy market behind the Exchequer, with three market houses, 'to which cheese, butter, pork, poultry, etc. are brought by women from the country.' The floating harbour had not yet been constructed and so at low tide the ships still lay on a bed of mud, and Southey described the busy quays with the view extending down the river into the

St Augustine's Back in 1826 with the River Frome completely uncovered. The tower in the foreground was a signalling beacon for approaching ships. Later it became a public convenience.

country. The cathedral, still without its nineteenth century nave, was, Southey thought, 'a poor building—excepting Chester, the least interesting in England.' He betrayed his acquaintance with Bristol by recording that the Bristol High Cross which had stood on College Green outside the Cathedral, had been removed, and that in 1768 it had been given to Sir Henry Hoare who re-erected it in his grounds at Stourhead. It is unlikely that a Spanish gentleman on a brief visit would have been sufficiently well-versed or interested in Bristol history to record that

"A fine cross, which formerly stood in the square, has been sold by the corporation to a gentleman, who has re-erected it at his country seat, and thus rescued it from destruction. This was about thirty years ago . . ."

Like many others, Southey enthused over the situation of Bristol and the beauties of the surrounding countryside.

"The views in the neighbourhood of this city are singularly pleasing. The adjoining village of Clifton was once the most beautiful village in England, and may now be said to be the finest suburb."[1]

94

It had for long been the practice for families who had grown rich through trade and commerce in Bristol to establish themselves in opulent mansions in the surrounding countryside though still within easy reach of the city. Thus the Smyth family who had made a fortune as Bristol merchants during the sixteenth century set themselves up as country gentry at Ashton Court; during the seventeenth century Bristol merchants like Sir Robert Cann took up residence at Stoke Bishop, Sir Robert Yeamans at Redland, and the Southwell family moved to Kings Weston where early in the eighteenth century Sir John Vanbrugh designed a grand new mansion for them on a tremendous and ostentatious scale. Likewise the copper smelter William Reeves built the romantic Gothick *extravaganza* at Arnos Court, and numerous merchant families left central Bristol for the heights of Clifton during the eighteenth century.

Among such families were the Harfords, a family of Quaker merchants and bankers, who purchased the Blaise Castle estate in the parish of Henbury in 1789, and built Blaise Castle House in 1796. What distinguishes the Harfords, however, is not their fine house and beautifully landscaped grounds, but the fact that in 1810-11 John Scandrett Harford employed John Nash to design the group of estate cottages which became known as Blaise Hamlet, and which had an enormous effect on the whole nineteenth century movement for the construction of picturesque cottages and romantic model villages. An early visitor to Blaise Castle Hamlet was J. N. Brewer who in 1824 published *Delineations of Gloucestershire* containing the following description of the Hamlet:

"Blaise Castle.
We have still to notice a very pleasing feature of this demesne. The grounds attached to the mansion are adorned with a lovely group of cottages, known by the name of BLAISE HAMLET. These cottages are ten in number, and were erected about the year 1810, by the late John S. Harford, Esq., father of the present proprietor, as retreats for aged persons, who had moved in respectable walks of life, but had fallen under misfortunes, preserving little, or nothing, in the shock of adversity, but unblemished character. The buildings evince no ostentation of charity, and would seem designed as elegant, though humble, places of voluntary retirement, rather than as the refuge of the needy, bestowed by the hand of neighbouring affluence. They were built after the designs of Mr Nash, and

95

constitute a collection of practical studies in romantic cottage architecture. A terrace-walk, of a wavy outline, leads along the front of the buildings, and encloses a lawn that called for no operation of art, but was left undulating by the hand of nature. Ivy, woodbine, jessamine, and various simple flowering plants, cling to these tenements of peace, and impart to them a beautiful and appropriate dressing. As a picturesque object, this hamlet is, indeed, a gem of prodigious value to the domain . . . since the smiling village, that adds to the picturesque attractions of the territory, at the same time forms a memorial of the founder's exemplary benevolence."[2]

One of the most robust as well as informative descriptions of the west country during the early nineteenth century was made by William Cobbett in his *Rural Rides*. Unfortunately Cobbett's visit to Bristol in July 1830 was cut short by the death of the King, George IV, and Cobbett cancelled the lectures he was to have given in the city. Nonetheless before he left he wrote a brief but characteristically energetic account of Bristol and Bristolians:

"Tour in the West   3 July 1830

Just as I was closing my third lecture (on Saturday night) at Bristol, to a numerous and most respectable audience, the news of the above event (the death of George IV) arrived. I had advertised and made the preparations for lecturing at Bath on Monday, Tuesday and Wednesday; but under the circumstances, I thought it would not be proper to proceed thither for that purpose, until after the burial of the king. When that has taken place I shall, as soon as may be, return to Bath, taking Hertfordshire and Buckinghamshire in my way; from Bath, through Somerset, Devon and into Cornwall; and back through Dorset, South Wilts, Hants, Sussex, Kent, and then go into Essex, and, last of all, into my native county of Surrey. I shall then have seen all England with my own eyes, except Rutland, Westmoreland, Durham, Cumberland, and Northumberland, and these, if I have life and health till next spring, I shall see in my way to Scotland. But never shall I see another place to interest me, and so pleasing to me, as Bristol and its environs, taking the whole together. A good and solid and wealthy city: a people of plain and good manners; private virtue and public spirit united; no empty noise, no insolence, no flattery; men very much like the Yorkers and Lancastrians. And as to the seat of the city and its environs, it surpasses all that I ever saw. A great commercial city in the midst of corn-fields, meadows and woods, and the ships coming into the centre of it, miles from anything like sea, up a narrow river, and passing between two clefts of a rock probably a hundred feet high; so that from the top of these clefts you *look down* upon the main-topgallant masts of lofty ships that are gliding along!"[3]

Throughout the early nineteenth century as for many previous centuries the great Bristol markets and fairs continued to be important in the commercial life of the whole of the West country and for much of the south of Wales. Butter, meat, fish and vegetables came into the city from the neighbouring counties and were brought by barges or 'trows' down the Severn and from Wales. A hay market was established in Broadmead, and droves of cattle and sheep were sold at the Thursday market held in St Thomas Street. The two fairs held originally on the feasts of St Paul (25 January) and St James (25 July) attracted dealers and customers from long distances, and the city became crowded with farmers, dealers, pedlars, cheap jacks and hawkers. The experience of the Rev. John Skinner, the antiquarian rector of Camerton near Bath, who came to Bristol during the summer of 1830, was typical. He wrote in his Journal,

"As we purposed to reach Bristol, being under the escort of Mr Richardson who had business there in the evening, and is acquainted with every part of this vast and dirty city, I did not wish to interfere as to our station for the night, but only requested we should take up with cleanly quarters if possible. The first inn we asked to be accommodated at was without success, as we had the mortification to find the morrow was the first day of Bristol Fair. At the second inn we stopped, they agreed to give us beds, but alas! I had reason to regret that which fell to my share, as it was so abundant in vermin. I could not close my eyes until their supper was concluded; and as soon as it was properly light I was glad to leave my bed and wash off as much as possible the pollutions to which I had been subject during the night."[4]

Overleaf: Donne's plan of Bristol 1826, showing the new developments of Clifton, Kingsdown, Redcliffe and Queen's Square. Whiteladies Road and Stokes Croft are roads into the country.

97

In the autumn of 1831, the year when Bristol was torn by quarrels and disturbances over various local issues, economic decline, unemployment and poverty, and above all, over the question of Parliamentary reform which was to lead to the spectacular Bristol riots of October 1831, the celebrated poet George Crabbe visited Clifton. He was captivated by the beauty of Clifton and of the Avon gorge, and wrote:

"I look from my window upon the Avon and its wooded and rocky bounds the trees yet green. A vessel is sailing down, and here comes a steamer (Irish, I suppose). I have in view the end of the Cliff to the right, and on my left a wide and varied prospect over Bristol, as far as the eye can reach, and at present the novelty makes it very interesting. Clifton was always a favourite place with me . . ."

Following the riots of 29th to 31st October in which the Bishop's palace was sacked and much of Queen Square burnt, Crabbe wrote:

"Bristol, I suppose, never in the most turbulent times of old witnessed such an outrage. Queen Square is but half standing, half is a smoking ruin."

The Bristol Riots of October 1831 were an uncharacteristically violent episode in Bristol's history, and ironically the Reform Act when it was passed by Parliament in 1832 had little effect on the sort of persons who formed the majority of the rioters. The destruction, burning and pillage caused by the rioters were widespread, including attacks on the Bridewell and the New Gaol, the burning of the Bishop's Palace next to the Cathedral, the burning and looting of the Mansion House and Custom House in Queen Square and widespread looting elsewhere. The Rev. Robert Gray, nephew of the Bishop of Bristol, was in the Bishop's Palace on 30 October 1831 when it was attacked, and wrote to the Home Secretary, Lord Melbourne, describing how the mob had forced an entry and

"Within a short space of twenty minutes, the palace, with its valuable furniture, books, etc., was in flames."

He continued that

"The City of Bristol is at present entirely in the possession of an organised *Banditti*, of the very vilest and yet of a most dastardly description . . ."

He urged the strongest action if the mob was to be prevented from taking over the whole city. Later that night his prediction proved true as the mob attacked, burned and looted the houses in Queen's

Square from which they were only cleared belatedly by a detachment of Dragoon Guards, with heavy loss of life and many injuries among the rioters. Others were burnt in the fires which they themselves had started, or were too drunk with stolen liquor to escape from the burning buildings crashing around them. The sight of the burning houses in Queen's Square and the fearful scenes of total lawlessness and anarchy in the heart of the city had a tremendous effect upon the citizens, and the fires could be seen for miles around. Charles Kingsley who was then twelve years old and a pupil at a school on St Michael's Hill had a good view over the city and later wrote that

> "The flames increased multiplied at one point after another; till, by ten o'clock that night, one seemed to be looking down upon Dante's *Inferno,* and to hear the multitudinous moan and wail of the lost spirits surging to and fro amid that sea of fire ... dull explosions down below mingled with the roar of the mob, and the infernal hiss and crackle of the flame."

In 1852 the popular mid-Victorian novelist and dramatist, Mary Russell Mitford, visited Bristol, and found it much more attractive than she had expected, and in many ways more interesting and varied than Bath. She even found Brunel's half-finished Suspension Bridge remarkably graceful, with a basket hung on the wires stretched between the two towers in which the Bridge Trustees allowed those who were bold enough to do so to cross the Gorge, the small sum which they were charged providing a small income for the Trustees during the long period when no work was done on the bridge. The Suspension Bridge was finally completed as a memorial to Brunel in 1864, six years after his death.

> "From Bath we proceeded to Bristol ... Of Bath, its buildings and its scenery, I had heard much good; of Bristol, its dirt, its dinginess, and its ugliness much evil. Shall I confess—dare I confess, that I was charmed with the old city? The tall, narrow, picturesque dwellings with their quaint gables; the wooden houses in Wine Street ... the courts and lanes climbing like ladders up the steep acclivities; the hanging gardens, said to have been given by Queen Elizabeth to the washerwomen, (everything has a tradition in Bristol), the bustling quays; the crowded docks; the calm silent Dowry Parade (I have my own reasons for loving Dowry Parade) with its trees growing up between the pavement like the close of a cathedral; the Avon

101

flowing between those two exquisite boundaries, the richly tufted Leigh Woods clothing the steep hill side, and the grand and lofty St Vincent's Rocks, with houses perched upon the summits that looked ready to fall upon our heads; the airy line of the chain that swung from tower to tower of the intended suspension bridge, with its basket hanging in mid air like the car of a balloon, making one dizzy to look at it; formed an enchanting picture. I know nothing in English landscape so lovely or so striking as that bit of the Avon beyond the Hot Wells, especially when the tide is in, the ferry boat crossing, and some fine American ship steaming up the river.''

During her stay in Bristol Mary Russell Mitford was escorted over the new steamship *The Great Britain* being built in Bristol to the designs of Isambard Kingdom Brunel. She also visited some of the Bristol churches including St Mary Redcliffe.

A noted Bristolian of the later nineteenth century who has left several descriptions of the city and its neighbourhood, was the scholar and historian of the Italian Renaissance John Addington Symonds. His father had been a leading Bristol physician, and in 1851 the family had moved from Berkeley Square to Clifton Hill House, the mansion which had been built in 1747 by the Bristol merchant, Paul Fisher. John Addington Symonds loved this fine house with its superb views across the Avon to Dundry Hill and Long Ashton:

"It is a ponderous square mansion, built for perpetuity with walls three feet in thickness, faced with smooth Bath stone. But, passing to the southern side, one still enjoys the wonderful prospect which I have described. Time has done much to spoil the landscape. Mean dwellings have clustered around the base of Brandon Hill, and crept along the slopes of Clifton. The city has extended on the further side towards Bedminster. Factory chimneys with their filth and smoke have saddened the simple beauty of the town and dulled the brightness of its air. But the grand features of nature remain. The rolling line of hills from Lansdown over Bath, through Dundry with its solitary church tower to Ashton guarding the gorge of Avon, presents a free and noble space for cloud shadows, a splendid

Opposite: Clifton Hill House, home of John Addington Symonds in the 19th century.

scene for the display of sunrise. The water from the Severn still daily floods the river-beds of Frome and Avon; and the ships still come to roost like ocean birds beside the ancient churches.''

A frequent visitor to Clifton Hill House was Symonds' friend and former tutor Benjamin Jowett, master of Balliol College and a passionate advocate for the spread of higher education. It was Jowett who played a leading part in the movement which led to the establishment of a University College in Bristol in 1876.

Most of the visitors to Bristol whose comments and impressions of the city have so far been quoted came on brief visits in search of health, recreation or business and described only their immediate reactions to Bristol and its neighbourhood. The nineteenth century was to see a whole stream of visitors of a very different sort who recorded the results of detailed and systematic enquiries into the city and people. These were the inspectors appointed by Parliament to collect evidence about many different subjects ranging from industries to sanitation, and from the medical condition and welfare of the poor to church life and religious education.

Few subjects were outside the concern of Parliament or escaped the scrutiny of Parliamentary inspectors, and the results of their enquiries were published in the form of Royal Commission reports, Select Papers of both Houses of Parliament or as Parliamentary Papers or 'Blue Books'. This mass of evidence gives a very different and far more detailed picture of Bristol than that provided by the impressions of casual visitors, and dwells on aspects of the life of the city that were generally ignored by other writers. The Parliamentary papers, Royal Commission Reports and the published reports of other official investigations provide one of the most fruitful and detailed sources of information on local history.

The evidence they provide shows the dramatic increase in the population of Bristol during the nineteenth century; even when suburbs which were not officially incorporated into the city until the end of the century are included, the population was less than 70,000 in 1801, while by 1851 it had grown to 160,000, and had reached 337,000 by 1901, an increase of more than 380% over the century as a whole. Although this was less than the staggeringly large increases of the newly developed nineteenth century towns such as Manchester, Liverpool, Birmingham or Middlesborough, it did nonetheless bring enormous problems to Bristol—slums, overcrowding, and an appalling mortality rate as public services such as sewage disposal and water supply completely failed to keep pace with the expanding demand, and Bristol became an extremely unhealthy and disease-ridden city. The stench of raw sewage from the Avon and the Frome, the lack of pure water and the overcrowded slums of the central area where the most elementary precautions to prevent disease were disregarded, ensured that by the mid-nineteenth century Bristol had a death rate surpassed only by Liverpool and Manchester.

At the same time the economy of Bristol and of the port declined rapidly from the prosperous years of the eighteenth century. Although improved dock facilities were provided between 1804 and 1809 when the floating harbour was constructed, thereby ensuring that ships were no longer deposited on the mud at low tide and that cargoes could be handled whatever the state of the tide, nonetheless the very high harbour dues charged in Bristol as compared with Liverpool or London, the inefficient running of the city docks and the decline in the traditional west-country industries such as woollen cloth, all these and numerous other factors contributed to the rapid decline in the trade of Bristol.

The sharp decline in the national importance of Bristol was already evident in 1828 when the annual publication Matthew's *Bristol Directory* noted that:

"Bristol for centuries ranked as the second city in England in respect of riches, trade and population; but the present extent of its foreign commerce will bear no comparison with that of the port of Liverpool; and it appears to be exceeded in population by the manufacturing town of Manchester . . ."[5]

The results of the declining prosperity of the city were dramatically illustrated by its sanitary condition. The traditional outlet for Bristol drains and the normal receptacle for the household refuse of the town had been the two rivers Avon and Frome. The rapid rise in population during the early nineteenth century greatly increased the amount of effluent and rubbish just at the time that the creation of the floating harbour meant that the rivers were no longer daily scoured by the tides. The results were horrific. The stench from the floating harbour was overpowering, and, not surprisingly, the central area of the town became an increasingly unhealthy place in which to live. The rich could escape to Clifton or to the rapidly expanding suburbs, though even in these places, there was inadequate

The River Frome near Lewin's Mead: "it may be considered as a great open sewer". Today, this is the site of large anonymous office blocks.

drainage and a shortage of pure water; but for the poor who were compelled to live close to the harbour, conditions became steadily more appalling throughout the first half of the nineteenth century.

Eventually in 1845 Parliament commissioned a *Report on the Sanatory Condition of Bristol* as part of a wider enquiry into the *Health of Large Towns and Populous Districts.* The Bristol report was written by two inspectors, Sir Henry de la Beche and Dr Lyon Playfair, and their comments show vividly a very different aspect of Bristol than that presented by polite visitors:

"The whole of the sewerage, anterior to the construction of the Floating-harbour, in 1809, was arranged for delivery into a tidal river, so that when the new cut was made from Hotwells to St Philip's Marsh, for the passage of the Avon, and the old course of the river between these points was converted into a Floating-harbour, nearly the whole sewerage of the city, as regarded its delivery into the tidal river, was disorganised, and the sewage thrown into the stagnant waters of the Floating-harbour."

The Report goes on to describe in graphic detail the evil smells which were emitted from the stagnant waters during warm weather and the reluctance over many years of the Dock Company and other public bodies to do anything to remedy the situation. It also provides horrific details of the large sewers all along the Floating harbour delivering raw sewage into the water:

"The course of the Frome, after that river enters among the houses of the town, may be regarded as the chief sewage nuisance in Bristol. Into it is discharged a large mass of the filth of the town, and it may be considered as a great open sewer . . . When the waters of the Frome are low, as generally happens in summer and autumn, the stench from the course of the Frome is great, and the inhabitants of the houses adjoining it, mostly of the poorer class, as scarcely any others will live in them, describe it as at times making them turn sick . . ."

The Commissioners reported that although the streets were generally reasonably clean, the state of the many courts and alleys was disgusting. They also described the squalid conditions in the courts and alleys of Temple district, Redcliffe, Lewin's Mead and St Philips:

"In Clifton, although chiefly composed of handsome houses, inhabited by persons in affluent and easy circumstances, the want of proper sewerage is deplorable. Ranges of handsome houses, otherwise well appointed, have nothing but a system of cesspools—often the holes from which the stones for building the chief and rough parts of the houses have been taken. There is indeed a sewer down two-thirds of the Royal Crescent, with one from Caledonia-place, falling into another from Sion-hill, which seems also to drain part of Prince's-buildings in its passage over the cliffs to the river. A sewer comes down from Savill-place and houses adjacent; passing down by Berkeley-place and Woodwell-lane to the float (i.e. floating harbour); but the mass of houses in Clifton has no sewerage."

Although earlier visitors such as Leland in the sixteenth century had praised the abundant supply of fresh water which was supplied to all parts of Bristol, the situation was very different in the nineteenth century. The chief supply of water was obtained from wells, and many of these were inadequate or were situated by cesspools or sewage outlets and were contaminated:

> "The water from the ancient well or pump of St Peter . . . in red sandstone, is considered better for making tea than those near it; a character perhaps due to the percolation to it of the filthy waters of the Frome and Float . . . When the Float was drained this well became dry . . . Viewed as a sanatory question, there are few, if any, large towns in England in which the supply of water is so inadequate as at Bristol."

Water closets were to be found only in the houses of the wealthy: in the poorer districts the Commissioners found few privies and these were often in bad repair and filthy, seldom cleaned. In some places there was an average of three privies to fourteen houses, and in many places the supply was even more scanty. Along the Frome the privies were built out over the river and discharged directly into it, and in summer when the water was low the whole course of the river became a stinking ditch 'and is disgusting in the extreme' or

> "It is too loathsome to describe. When the tide comes up, matters are, for a time, still worse; for it comes loaded with the filth discharged from the sewers that open further down. The stench then becomes almost intolerable."

They also commented at length upon the general uncleanliness of the people and their houses, the overcrowded conditions and the neglect of elementary hygiene. After their detailed, painstaking and often distasteful enquiries into the sanitation of Bristol, the Commissioners concluded sadly that because of the total neglect of the most elementary and basic sanitary precautions,

> "Bristol, with a climate known to be mild and salubrious, enjoys the unenviable celebrity of being the third most unhealthy town in England."[6]

An inevitable result of the appallingly low standards of hygiene, poor and contaminated water-supply, overcrowded housing and totally inadequate drainage in many parts of Bristol, was that there were frequent epidemics and that cholera and typhoid were regular visitors to the city. In 1848-49 for example, nearly 15,000 Bristolians were treated for fever and diaorrhoea and 789 were confirmed as suffering from cholera; of them 445 died. A Report to the House of Commons (General Board of Health) in 1850 by one of the Commissioners, Mr Goldney, reported that the chief cause in Bristol was bad or non-existent public works:

"The drainage was in many places positively injurious to public health, and the state of the water-supply and privies in the affected localities perhaps worse than I have seen it in most other places."

He also reported that

"the outbursts of cholera were chiefly confined to well-marked, defined, bad localities, and along the banks of the river Frome."[7]

Slowly and gradually the sanitary condition of central Bristol improved, an Improvement Committee of the City Council was set up in 1840, and in 1846 the Bristol Water Works Company was established by Act of Parliament and began the formidable task of bringing pure water to the city from the Chew valley area of Somerset. The first supply of water along the fifteen miles of pipeline reached Bristol in June 1850, and although at first only a comparatively few houses were supplied, slowly the situation improved and pure water became widely available. Meanwhile a Sanitary Committee had been appointed by the City Council and through their Inspectors began the laborious struggle to provide adequate drains and sewers, and to abolish nuisances such as foul cesspools, filthy pig-stys and dung-heaps, and insanitary slaughter-houses. Slowly the streets were improved, paved and cleared of mud and filth while the number of crowded and disease-ridden courts and alleys was gradually reduced. The result of this work was a substantial improvement in public health in Bristol, and between 1851 and 1869 the annual mortality rate in the city fell from 28 per thousand in 1851 to 22 per thousand in 1869. Much of this improvement was due to the dedicated work of Bristol doctors, and especially to the efforts of William Budd (1811-1880), a Bristol doctor who studied the causes and the spread of cholera and typhoid in the city, and as physician to the Bristol Royal Infirmary and a lecturer at the Bristol Medical College was an active pioneer in pressing the urgent need for better sanitary conditions. But progress was nonetheless slow, and it was not until another epidemic of typhus swept through the poorer parts of the city in 1864 that the corporation appointed Dr David Davies as its first Medical Officer of Health. The mortality rate in Bristol did, however, slowly improve, as is shown by the following figures for annual deaths per thousand persons in the city:

109

1876	22.6
1877	22.5
1878	22.2
1879	21.9
1880	21.0
1881	19.6
1882	19.1
1883	17.9

In evidence to the *Royal Commissions on the Housing of the Working Classes* in 1884-5, the Medical Officer of Health for Bristol, Dr David Davies, attributed this decline in the mortality rate to three causes. First, the making of new sewers throughout the city, and he stated that since 1852 no fewer than 150 miles of sewers had been laid; second, the new supply of copious quantities of pure water from the Mendip Hills; and third, the efforts of his staff of sanitary inspectors in preventing and stopping filth, nuisances, overcrowding and disease-producing squalor.

A fruitful source of information on local industries during the nineteenth century is derived from the reports of the many inspectors who visited the city to collect evidence for another series of parliamentary enquiries. Many of these reports give detailed evidence about industries, industrial processes, machinery, conditions of work, wages and the welfare of employees. For example, considerable details about conditions underground at Bedminster colliery can be found in the evidence collected by Dr Leonard Stewart in 1842 on the employment of children. The manager, Moses Reynolds, told him that boys were employed underground from the age of eight years, and were used in opening and shutting doors to regulate the current of air. They worked 12 hours a day and received 4d a day. Slightly older boys were employed at piece-work as 'carriage-boys' to 'shove the coal along the level in the carts or "hudges".' The low galleries were, he said, very damp and cold, and were lit by candles. Elsewhere, in north Somerset and south Gloucestershire, Dr Stewart reported on the use of the "guss and crook", the belt and strap used by boys to pull carts along the cramped mine tunnels, but he was told by miners that the boys were not injured by this curious harness. The manager reported that the colliers were generally uneducated and could not read or write, though a few of the boys attended Sunday school, and

"they commonly drink a good deal, and particularly on Saturdays and Sundays. They generally keep a good deal together and marry among their own people—having usually large families."[8]

Among the workers who were interviewed by Dr Stewart was George Raikes aged 11 years who worked at the Marsh Pit. He had started work at 9 years old, but stated that there were boys of 7 and 8 working in the pit. He began work at 6.00 am and finished at 4.00 or 5.00 pm, and was employed as a 'carriage-boy'. He found it 'rather hard work and gets tired sometimes'. He was paid at piecework and generally earned 7d per day. He had holidays at Christmas and Whitsuntide.

In 1843 Dr Leonard Stewart again visited Bristol, this time to collect information for a parliamentary enquiry into trades and manufactures. His report reveals the large number of small factories and workshops tightly crammed into houses, courts and yards in the central area of Bristol, the large number of unskilled labourers employed especially women and girls, and the very long hours which were regarded as normal. For example, at Acraman's Iron-foundry he found many boys employed aged from 12 years, and working a twelve hour day; at the Bristol Pottery of Messrs. Poutney and Goldney 225 people were employed of whom a half were under 18 years of age. There were 75 women and 50 children of 10 or 11 years of age; all worked a twelve hour day from 6 am to 6 pm. Dr Stewart interviewed some of the children, and his notes on two of them were as follows:

"Matilda Bennett, aged 11, examined April 30th 1841.
Is a 'painting girl' at the 'Bristol Pottery'. Has been so 'about a two years'. Paints cups and saucers. Comes from six to six o'clock, with half an hour for breakfast and one hour for dinner. Sits at her work; and is employed every day when there is work. Is under Mr Marsh, the foreman, who superintends, but 'never beats her or treats her ill'. Is paid as much as she earns, and gets 4s 6d a week at the most, and sometimes 2s 9d and 2s 0d. 'Has her health very well' and likes her work and treatment.

Sarah Hazel, aged 12:
Is a cutter at the 'Bristol Pottery'. Cuts the patterns, and 'begins at six and leaves at six'. Is never beaten, 'only scolded if she does not do her work'. Works under Henry Cole. There is no accident or injury to which she is exposed from the work

itself. Cannot read or write, but goes to a Sunday-school, and can spell.''

Dr Stewart also visited Rickett's Flint-glass works, and various milliners and dress-makers. The latter employed large numbers of women and girls who worked exceedingly long hours, 'in the busy season (or from May through the summer) from five or six in the morning till twelve at night'. The work was sedentary, trying on the eyes and poorly-paid.

Another of the parliamentary commissioners, Elijah Waring, visited Bristol in 1843 to enquire into trades and manufactures. He visited Acraman's 'Locomotive Engine and General Iron Manufactory' in St Philip's where about 1,200 men and boys were employed, including 80 boys under thirteen years of age and another 120 under eighteen; the youngest boy was seven years old. All worked a twelve-hour day. He also visited other, smaller, foundries and iron manufactories in St Philip's, Marsh Street and Swan Court and the works of the Bristol Cut-Nail Company in Wilder Street where many boys of from nine years of age were employed to attend the nail-cutting machines.

> "The boys are chiefly sons of agricultural labourers, living several miles from the city. They bring their meals with them; usually bread and butter; rarely have any meat . . . They are a rather unmanageable set; and sometimes strike for more wages, when there is more than ordinary demand for their labour . . .''

At Two Mile Hill a Pin Manufactory employed 160 people, including 110 women and children, while another 500 women and children were employed in their own homes in putting the heads on the pins and packing them. Again, the hours of work were from 6 am to 6 pm. The commissioner found that in the factory:

> "A fine of 3d is inflicted on any female who uses bad language, or sings a profane song; they sing a great deal, but are permitted only hymn tunes, of which they have a great variety. There is no mode of discriminating in any other way between proper and improper subjects of melody.''[9]

In 1862 a further Commission on Children's Employment was es-

Opposite: Steep Street. Part of the network of shabby narrow streets, alleys and steps that climbed up from St Augustine's Back to St Michael's Hill. An area packed with primitive Victorian workshops and small factories.

tablished by Parliament, and as part of the enquiries of this Commission, interesting evidence on factories and workshops in Bristol was collected during 1865 by Mr J. Edward White. This report on Bristol shows clearly the very wide range of products which were made in Bristol, many of them in small workshops which were crowded into the central area of the city. Besides larger concerns such as collieries, glassworks, brickworks, ironworks, sugar refining, soap boiling and chemical works, there were many smaller trades and occupations such as metal working, brass, nail and pin making, lead works, chocolate-making, tobacco, printing, clothing trades, tanning, rag-picking and numerous others. Many of these trades were very labour-intensive, several employed a high proportion of low-paid female labour, and powered machinery played only a small part in their operations. The investigator, Edward White commented that:

"Bristol is a picturesque city, partly from its situation, but chiefly from the age and character of its streets and buildings, many of which have the look of belonging to the middle ages. This, however, has the natural drawbacks in narrow streets and inconvenient buildings . . ."

The worst places he found were the marine store sheds, where women were employed in sorting, tearing and cutting old rags to be used in paper and shoddy making.

"In these rags, paper picked from scavengers' carts, bones and all sorts of rubbish, of kinds which of course cause effluvia, are accumulated."

The investigator found the stench appalling and the atmosphere close and dusty.

Wages for children were stated to be from 3s to 5s per week, though a few received less. In spite of the very long hours of work, the inspector's general impression of working hours in Bristol was that, compared to many other places, they were 'moderate not exceeding 12', but he was concerned about the lack of education displayed by the children:

"But my general impression is, that in Bristol, as compared with many other places which I have visited, there is little of too early or excessive work of children or young people."

They were, however, very critical of the conditions in some of the factories and especially of the lack of adequate lavatories:

"In Bristol there is in general a great want of proper privy accommodation, not only in the dwelling houses of the poorer classes but also in the manufactories. The establishments in which females work are as badly off in this respect as others. There are commonly no waterclosets, but only one or two outdoor places common to all workers . . .

Thus in one place, where at least 150 persons of both sexes are employed, there are only two privies, and in another there is only one for 100 or 150 men and boys. These are merely instances of what is found all through the city. The places themselves are often choked up and in a filthy state . . ."

One establishment stood out from all the rest in the Report of 1866 for its cleanliness and for the care which was taken of the employees. This was the premises of Joseph Storrs Fry, chocolate and cocoa manufacturers, in Union Street. Like many other firms in the central area, Fry's premises were converted dwelling houses, and consisted of a large number of small rooms, but the inspector was greatly impressed by all he saw there:

"The evident care bestowed on the comfort and welfare of the people employed here is such as befits the well-known family name which the firm bears, and makes it a pleasure to visit the place. The rooms are airy and cheerful. Cleanliness prevails, and the women and girls' work is well suited for them. The younger girls whom I spoke to had all been at school and said that they could read, and some elder girls and young women sent down to me by the forewoman, without selection, all read nicely from a magazine, except one who made mistakes, as it seemed from nervousness. A room is set apart as a school room and chapel, at which I attended by invitation the short morning service, at which the Scriptures and a hymn are read, with explanations where necessary. It was pleasing to see the orderly way in which they came in and sat down, one by one, the little girls in front, then the elder and women, then the boys, and at the back the men, each taking down their Bibles from shelves as they entered. I was much struck with the general attention shown throughout the service. Though it was 8.45 am and therefore after work had been going on for some time, all came in as bright and fresh looking as if at a Sunday school, except that the clean canvas jackets of the men and boys and aprons of girls showed that it was a working day . . ."

Some 200 persons were employed at Frys, two-thirds of them

View from Brandon Hill in 1842, from almost the same position as Buck's in 1734. The smoking chimneys of the industrial revolution had clouded the horizon.

women and girls, and about seventy were girls under the age of 18. The men and boys worked from 6 am to 6 pm, while the women and girls worked from 8 am to 6 pm. Joseph Storrs Fry explained this by saying that:

> "We found it better to let them take their breakfast comfortably at home before they come to work, instead of stopping for it afterwards."

He emphasised the care which was taken of the health and comfort of the workpeople, and especially of the young, and also stated that:

> "No persons, however skilful, are retained whose moral conduct is unsatisfactory."[10]

By the late nineteenth century the great growth in the population of Bristol had spread streets and houses, shops and factories, far beyond the boundaries of the medieval town, and the real area of the city extended for several miles into the former countryside of Gloucestershire and Somerset. In 1894, and again in 1897, the area of Bristol was extended, increasing its area from 4,461 to 11,500 acres, and the population of the urban area had reached 356,000 by 1900. Parishes to the east of the city, St Paul, St George and St Philip, as well as the Gloucestershire parishes of Mangotsfield and Stapleton, had become increasingly industrialised and heavily-populated during the later nineteenth century, and there had been massive residential and industrial development south of the Avon in Brislington, St Anne's and Bedminster, while the population of the city-centre parishes had declined before the growth of shops and offices. In 1877 the first dock was made at Avonmouth to provide berths for larger ships which could not navigate the twisting, difficult course of the Avon and reach the city docks. In 1884 the Corporation of Bristol took over the Avonmouth docks and thus secured control of the whole port of Bristol, and in 1908 the Royal Edward dock was opened, an enormous and impressive civic project, capable of accommodating the largest vessels then afloat. In 1910 Sir George White founded the Bristol Aeroplane Company at Filton and thus began the close involvement of Bristol with the new aircraft industry, an association which was to have profound effects for the future.

Notes
1. J. Simmons (ed.) *Letters from England by Robert Southey* 1951. pp. 475-83.
2. J. N. Brewer *Delineations of Gloucestershire*, 1824, p. 108.
3. William Cobbett *Rural Rides*, Everyman Edition, 1912, II, p. 276.
4. H. Coombs and A. N. Bax (eds.), *Journal of a Somerset Rector*, 1930, p. 255.
5. *Matthew's Bristol Directory*, 1828, 196.
6. Sir Henry de la Beche, *Report on the state of Bristol* 1845, made for *Royal Commission on the state of Large Towns & Populous districts*.
7. *General Report to the Board of Health on the Cholera Epidemic*, 1848-9, Parliamentary Papers, 1850 (1273-5).
8. *Report on the Employment of Children in Coal Mines*, Parliamentary Papers, 1842, XVI, XVII.
9. *Report on Trades and Manufactures*, Parliamentary Papers, 1843, XIV, XV.
10. *Report of the Commission on Children's Employment*, 1866, Parliamentary Papers, 1866, XXIV (3678).

Other Sources
David Large and Frances Round, *Public Health in Mid-Victorian Bristol*, Bristol Historical Association, 1974.
B. Little, *The City and County of Bristol*, 1954.
Stanley Hutton *Bristol and its Famous Associations*, 1907.
H. E. Meller, *Leisure and the Changing City*, 1976.
Royal Commission on the Health of Towns, 2nd Report, 1845, Parliamentary Papers, 1845, XVIII, Appendix.

SIX

EARLY TWENTIETH CENTURY
'A Genuine City, an Ancient Metropolis'

Although every aspect of life in Bristol during the twentieth century has been researched and investigated as never before, and although the growth in the city, the changes in the lives of Bristolians, the rise and fall of trades and industries, sport, religion, social conditions and every aspect of life and work have been measured, charted and published in great detail, the older tradition whereby visitors recorded their impressions of the city has almost completely died out.

The growth of the population of Bristol from less than 50,000 people in 1801 to some 330,000 in 1901, and to 440,000 by 1951, together with the massive spread of suburbs and housing estates, the increasingly vast size of industries and the growth of complex national and international undertakings such as the aircraft industry or chemical manufacture, the many similarities between all modern towns, and the massive complexities of a modern conurbation, all mean that it is no longer easily possible to comprehend the character and atmosphere of a city or to sum it up in a short passage. The result is that few writers have attempted to continue the old tradition of English topographical writing.

A detailed picture of Bristol at the beginning of the twentieth century is provided by a report produced by commissioners of the Board of Trade, who visited the city in 1908 to enquire into 'Working Class Rents, Housing and Retail Prices'. Their Report contains much more general information than its title might suggest, and provides an appropriate conclusion to this survey of the varied impressions of visitors to Bristol during the course of nine centuries. Like so many other visitors, the Commissioners of the Board of Trade commented upon the situation of Bristol and the trade of its port:

> "Bristol consists of a bottle-shaped strip of land stretching for some nine miles from south-east to north-west, and having a width varying from five or six miles to about a quarter of a mile. On the west it extends to the coast of St George's

Channel, but between the old city and the sea there is a long tract of agricultural land. Up to the early part of the 19th century it was the second port of the United Kingdom. Since then its relative importance has declined, but it is still the centre of a great foreign and coasting trade."

The Commissioners also commented upon the docks in the city centre, the docks at Avonmouth and Portishead and on the Royal Edward dock which was being constructed at Avonmouth to take the largest ships afloat. They reported that Bristol was an important grain-importing centre: in 1906, for example, 4¾ million tons of wheat were imported through the port of Bristol, 4 million tons of barley and over 3 million tons of maize:

"The huge square granary by the side of the city docks is significantly one of the most prominent buildings in the city."

Bristol also imported large quantities of petroleum and other oils, cheese and sugar and there was an important coastal trade.

"The growth of the city on the west having been hindered by the downs, expansion has taken place mainly to the south and east, and it is in these directions that the city becomes more and more markedly industrial in character."

The Commissioners were impressed by the great variety of industries and employments in Bristol. Production of boots and shoes, paper and printing, the making of paper bags and boxes, manufacture of cocoa and chocolate, the corrugated iron works which were the largest in the country, furniture making, engineering, vehicle construction, tobacco manufacture and corset making which was 'one of the chief openings for female labour in Bristol.'

Industrial distribution of the population of Bristol compiled from the Census of 1901

	Employees	
Trade	**Men**	**Women**
Railways	3,351	
Carmen, Carriers, Carters, etc.	3,721	
Dock & Wharf Labourers	2,121	
Gardeners, Nurserymen & Seedsmen	876	
Coal & Shale Mine Workers	1,460	
Engineering & Machine Making	4,412	
Arms & Miscellaneous Metal Trades	1,438	117
Vehicles	1,312	

Electrical Apparatus makers	354	
House-building, etc.	10,979	
Cabinet Makers, French Polishers, Upholsterers	1,649	103
Earthenware, China & Porcelain manufacture	242	118
Glass-bottle manufacture	215	
Oil Millers, Oil Cake makers	251	
Soap boilers	230	
Tanners	435	
Curriers, Leather Goods makers	280	
Saddle, Whip & Harness makers	245	
Brush & Broom makers	307	178
Paper box & bag & Stationery manufacture	272	1,805
Printers & Lithographers	1,914	152
Cotton & Flax manufacture	179	1,066
Boot, Shoe, Slipper, Patten and Clog-makers	4,558	1,769
Staymakers	160	1,655
Chocolate & Cocoa makers	944	1,567
Tobacco manufacture	903	2,966
Brewers	289	
Domestic Servants		11,977
Tailoresses		4,863
Milliners, Dressmakers		4,021

Turning to their main task of examining the housing rents and prices in Bristol, the Commissioners found that, compared to London or to many of the industrial cities of the north of England, conditions in Bristol were very good. Their Report shows a marked contrast with the conditions which had existed fifty years earlier, for they concluded that, apart from a few over-crowded and insanitary courts near the river in Bedminster, the working-class housing of Bristol was good and there was little over-crowding. Rents and prices they also found to be moderate, while wages were satisfactory and compared very favourably with those paid in London and elsewhere. One consequence of the improved housing, sanitation and water supply of Bristol was that public health had improved considerably. They reported that the Corporation maintained public baths, wash-houses, hospitals and cemeteries, and that it also controlled the electricity supply, and that adequate supplies of pure water were available throughout the city. As a result, the annual death rate per 1,000 persons had fallen from the alarmingly high figure of 23 or 24 during the mid-nineteenth century to 16 by the 1890s and to 14 by 1905. Their general conclusion therefore was that at the beginning of the twentieth century Bristol was a pleasant and agreeable place in which to live and work.

"The residential areas occupied by the working classes are to be found chiefly in the south and east. In the south is the district of Bedminster where, in the neighbourhood of the river, a number of narrow streets and courts exist, giving shelter to an impoverished class of people. The courts have frequently a certain quaintness; but though back-to-back houses here, as in the whole of Bristol, are rare, the air space around each house is often insufficient as judged by modern standards. The number of dwellings comprised in these old and defective areas is not large when considered in relation to the size of the city . . . The great bulk of the working-class dwellings in Bristol conform to two general types—the small plain-fronted house built direct from the pavement, and the large house with bay windows and a small forecourt. Houses of this description constitute the main residential feature of Bedminster, Easton and St George . . .

Overcrowding in Bristol is but slight when compared with the conditions in some other large centres of population."[1]

Between 1918 and 1939 Bristol changed more rapidly than in any previous period. Some old established industries such as glass making ceased to exist, coal mining greatly declined, and other manufacturers such as Fry's Chocolate moved out of the city. The growth of the docks at Avonmouth, where the Royal Edward Dock was greatly improved between 1922 and 1928, meant that new industries, notably engineering, aircraft, chemical manufacture and motor vehicle construction grew rapidly in importance.

In 1938 part of the river Frome in the city centre from Baldwin Street to the former Quay Head was covered over, and this, together with the huge new offices for the Electricity and Gas Boards, created the present appearance of the city centre, and meant that ships could no longer be tied up in the heart of the city.

Perhaps the most obvious change was the move of population from the old inner city areas such as the slums of St Philips to the new suburban housing estates. Between 1918 and 1939 15,000 houses were built on new Council estates encircling Bristol such as Knowle, Bedminster Down, Fishponds, Sea Mills, Speedwell, Horfield, St Annes and Southmead, while a further 21,000 new houses were constructed on new estates by private builders. Improved transport facilities meant a massive growth in middle-class commuters, many travelling daily to Bristol from Clevedon, Portishead, Weston-super-Mare, Thornbury, Keynsham or from the villages of north Somerset and south Gloucestershire. The growth of the University whose new buildings at the top of Park Street, the gift of the Wills family, were opened by George V in 1925, also provided much employment both in the main University complex and in the numerous halls of residence in Clifton.

In spite of the rapidity and scale of change and all the complexities of modern urban life, a few writers continued the old tradition of topographical description. In 1927 H. V. Morton published *In Search of England,* a personal view of the condition of England a decade after the Great War. He said little of Bristol, however, except to comment, as had so many travellers before, on the sight of the ships crowded into the heart of the city, and to remark on the long centuries of close association between Bristol and maritime adventure.

Much more in the manner of the old topographers was J.B. Priestley, already a famous author and playwright, who published his highly personal *English Journey* in 1934 giving an account of his impressions on travelling through England in the autumn of 1933. Within less than a decade much of the central area of Bristol which Priestley saw and loved was to be destroyed by German bombs, notably in the great raids of November 1940, and his description is therefore summarised here as a final impression of the old pre-war Bristol which was so soon to disappear.

Priestley was pleasantly surprised by Bristol, finding it a fine, agreeable city, totally unlike the industrial towns of the north of England with which he was familiar. He was excited by the fine buildings, the ancient streets, lanes and alleys, the crowded pavements and shops, the port, ships and pubs, and by the people, 'I feel that the working people here enjoy life,' he wrote, 'There is not that terrible dreariness which is probably the chief curse of our provincial towns.'

Above all, Priestley was impressed by the atmosphere of the city in 1933

"It is a genuine city, an ancient metropolis . . . The Merchant Venturers have vanished; the slave trade, on whose evil proceeds this city flourished once, is now only a reminder of man's cruelty to man; the port, depending on the shallow twisting Avon, is only a shadow of its old self; but Bristol lives on, indeed arrives at a new prosperity, by selling us Gold Flake and Fry's chocolate and soap and clothes and a hundred other things. And the smoke from a million gold flakes solidifies into a new Gothic Tower for the university; and the chocolate melts away only to leave behind it all the fine big shops down Park Street, the pleasant villas out at Clifton, and an occasional glass of Harvey's Bristol Milk for nearly everybody."[2]

The final destruction of much of the old, historic Bristol with its unique atmosphere of sea-port, metropolis, and industrial city, dominated by its church towers and everywhere providing reminders of the great days of its maritime prosperity, came during the German bombing raids of the Second World War. A total of 1,299 Bristolians were killed by bombs, and 3,305 were injured during 78 air raids. Above all, it was the six major air raids in 1942 which destroyed so much of the historic medieval heart of Bristol where ancient churches, public buildings, shops and offices and houses were closely crowded together, in an area which has never been rebuilt since that time.

All parts of the inner city were affected by bombing. Park Street, Queen's Road, the Prince's Theatre, the Great Hall of the University, Clifton parish church, St James Barton, St Philips, Bedminster and many other districts were badly damaged, and the effect on the ancient heart of the city was appalling. The area of Castle Street, Wine Street, Marsh Street, St Nicholas Street, High Street, Union Street and many others which had formed the core of the shopping area and busy social life of pre-War Bristol were totally destroyed. So too were the medieval churches of St Peter, St Mary-le-port, St Nicholas, the Temple together with the Dutch House and the beautiful Elizabethan building of St Peter's Hospital. An earlier, damaging raid occurred during the night of 11 April 1941, and by chance the Prime Minister, Winston Churchill, was in Bristol and in his capacity of Chancellor of the University was to present degrees on the next day. It is appropriate to end this survey of visitors' impressions of Bristol, therefore, with the reaction of the Prime Minister to the destruction of so much of the historic city, and the evidence it provides of the amazing resilience and courage of Bristolians under the worst series of catastrophes ever to affect their historic city.

After spending the night in a special train just outside Bristol, constantly disturbed by the sounds of bombing and anti-aircraft fire, the Prime Minister inspected the destruction and devastation and the still-burning fires of the city. In spite of their losses the people greeted the Prime Minister with great enthusiasm and fortitude, and the degree congregation went ahead as planned even though part of the University buildings were still in flames, and graduates were still wet and covered in grime from fire-fighting. Later Churchill again toured the damaged parts of the city, and some years later one of his aides, Lord Ismay, recalled that

> "People were still being dug out, but there was no sign of a faltering anywhere. Only efficiency and resolution. At one of the rest centres at which you called, there was a poor old woman who had lost all her belongings sobbing her heart out. But as you entered, she took her handkerchief from her eyes and waved it madly shouting 'Hooray, hooray'."[3]

As Churchill's train pulled out of Bristol station, and the last of the cheering crowds were gone, Averell Harriman noticed that tears filled the Prime Minister's eyes, and he picked up a newspaper to hide his face from those who were with him, choking through his emotion: 'They have such confidence. It is a grave responsibility.'

Notes

1. *Enquiry by the Board of Trade into Working Class Rents, Housing and Retail Prices*, 1908, Cd 3864, 117-125.
2. J. B. Priestley, *English Journey*, 1934, pp. 25-36.
3. Martin Gilbert, *Winston S. Churchill*, VI, 1939-41, 1983, p. 1059.

Other Sources

F.C. Jones *The Bristol Waterworks Company 1846-1946*, 1946
Mary Russell Mitford *Recollections of a Literary Life*, 1852, III, 1-2
Royal Commission on the Housing of the Working Classes, Parliamentary Papers 1884-5, C4402

Opposite: Previously unpublished pictures, from a contemporary newsreel, of Churchill's visit to Bristol in April 1941, after a particularly bad air raid.

INDEX

127

Bristol Books

Redcliffe are the leading publishers of books about Bristol, having produced over forty on different aspects of the city's life and history. The following are a small selection:

Bristol Between the Wars   Ed. David Harrison   £3.50

Bristol has never seen such years of change as those between the two World Wars, changes mirrored in this compelling account.

This frank, intimate book, richly illustrated with rare, archive photographs, captures a permanent record of a period rapidly slipping beyond personal experience.

Bristol: Maritime City by Frank Shipsides and Robert Wall   £10.00

The epic story of the Port of Bristol is recalled from the earliest times, when man first set out to tame the formidable Severn estuary through the turbulent centuries of English history right up to the current 20th century controversies over the new Royal Portbury Dock.

The book is essential reading for all lovers of Bristol, and for those who admire and seek to understand her greatness.

John Cabot by Bryan Little   £1.50

Authentic material about John Cabot, one of the great figures in Britain's maritime history, is very scarce. Drawing on largely inaccessible and out-of-print material, historian Bryan Little has brought together the genuine facts about Cabot's life and achievements in Italy, the Near East, Bristol and North America.

The Bristol Scene by Jennifer Gill   £1.25

A fascinating glimpse of how the city looked in the early nineteenth century, just before the advent of the camera.

Many of the illustrations are from the priceless Braikenridge Collection in the City Art Gallery. George Weare Braikenridge, a retired merchant and plantation owner, had antiquarian interests, and commissioned nearly 1,500 drawings by local artists of Bristol between 1818 and 1830.

The Bristol House by Keith Mallory   £6.50

A lavish survey of the riches of Bristol's domestic architecture. From medieval buildings, Georgian terraces, Victorian villas and artisan terraces, through to the twentieth century and contemporary design. Over 130 illustrations.